# DARIEN WATERS

By and with
# Bobbi Phelps

SKY RANCH
Living on a Remote Ranch in Idaho

SAVING FRANKIE
Adventures of a Rescued Barn Cat

BLACK EMPRESS
Rescuing a Puppy from Iran

BEHIND THE SMILE
During the Glamour Years of Aviation

WRITES OF PASSAGE 2011

FLYFISHING ALWAYS

# DARIEN
# WATERS

## Following the Formative Years
## of a Darien Descendant

*For Betsy & Mark – Enjoy the latest memoir. 5/8/21*
*2 Bobbi*

## BOBBI PHELPS

*B Phelps*

All inquiries should be addressed to:

Village Concepts, 124 Chota Shores Way, Loudon, TN 37774.

Library of Congress Control Number 2021906445

Names: Phelps, Bobbi, author. Phelps, Barbara, author.

Title: Darien Waters / Bobbi Phelps.

Description: Phelps, Bobbi – Family. Darien, Connecticut.

Women – Biography. Author – American. Coming of Age. Christian Biography. Anecdotes.

Print ISBN: 978-1-63821-000-9

Ebook ISBN: 978-1-63821-001-6

Printed in the United States of America by Village Concepts, L.L.C. Visit Bobbi's website at www.booksbybobbi.com.

The website for the Authors Guild of Tennessee, of which Bobbi is a past president: www.authorsguildoftn.org.

Cover Design of the Rings End Bridge by Bob Ballard and Cheryl Peyton. Photo supplied by Getty Images.

Lindley Murray Franklin was the designer of the Rings End Bridge and grandfather to Gaysie and Janet Franklin, classmates of mine, and John Franklin, a classmate of my older sister. The stone bridge was built in 1930 near Gorham's Pond. Its three arches, beautiful and beckoning, graces the mouth of Goodwives River.

# DEDICATED
## to
## MY PARENTS:

Florence Winmill Bassford Phelps
and James Fielding Phelps

## and to
## MY SISTERS:

Virginia Lee Phelps Clemens
and Mary Gail Phelps Champlin

*They encouraged me, influenced me, and challenged me.*
*I'm blessed to have had them in my life.*

# DISCLAIMER

*Darien Waters* reflects the recollections of my hometown experiences between 1943 and 1962; adventures that took place at an innocent time before automobile seatbelts, bicycle helmets, cellphones, and computers. It was also a time when African-Americans were designated as "colored."

The conversations written on the following pages have been recreated to evoke the substance of what was said. While all the incidents described in this book are true to the best of my memory, certain events have been compressed, consolidated, or rearranged to aid in the narrative flow. *Darien Waters* is not intended to be an exact duplication but an effective representation of a young woman's coming of age in an upscale town along Connecticut's "gold coast."

# AUTHOR'S NOTE

Most names mentioned in *Darien Waters* are correct and have been proofread and approved by the specifically-noted individual. Because of the lapse of time, however, I have forgotten several names. Or I surmised that the actual person would dislike being identified. For these two reasons, I have included several pseudonyms. They are in alphabetical order: Angelo, Brenda, Debby, Eddie, Enzo, Frank, Hannah, Jenny, Jerry, Manny, *Midnight Manor*, Millie, Miss Banks, Mrs. Jones, Mrs. Milano, and Roy.

*Bobbi Phelps*

# PROLOGUE

Reflecting simpler times, *Darien Waters* is a portrait of a young woman maturing from toddler to teenager in a Connecticut community, exposing both her failures and triumphs. Vivid and dramatic, yet anchored in seemingly everyday activities, *Darien Waters* is a narrative sweep that's both informative and entertaining.

During the 1940s and 1950s, almost every major American company had its headquarters in New York City. Their executives lived within an eighty-mile radius and traveled mostly by train from New Jersey, New York, Pennsylvania, and Connecticut. With a population of almost 10,000 in 1943, Darien was one of those commuter towns. Among the more famous residents were the Charles Lindbergh family, Margaret Burke-White (first female war photojournalist), and Leslie Groves (military head of the Manhattan Project).

It was during this time when long-distance telephone calls were made on Sundays, clothes and cars were purchased with cash, dimes were kept for payphones and bathrooms, and children ran outside with abandon. Parents turned their offspring loose to roam the fields and woods, to bicycle to the beach, and to wander into neighbors' houses. Invited or not. Young kids had no plans or schedules, nothing except to return home for meals. They were left to their own devices without a parent in sight. Their imaginations ran rampant as they created fantasy objects out of nothing.

My father, a commercial real estate manager, commuted to New York City, volunteered at the local fire department, belonged to the University Club in Manhattan, and was a charter member of the Country Club of Darien. He taught me to work hard, to obey rules, and to keep my word. My mother, a free-spirited individual, seemed to have few boundaries. She volunteered at Hindley Elementary, the Girl Scouts, the Darien Community Association, and for Planned Parenthood. She taught her children to explore, to question, and to learn. She was forever curious and was the ultimate optimist who never gossiped.

What follows are amusing, historical, and sometimes uncomfortable, accounts of my life in one of the most beautiful, waterside towns of Connecticut.

# TODDLER TIMES
## 1943 – 1945

# THE POND ON LEROY AVENUE

The backdoor slammed and our china plates rattled high above in the kitchen cabinets. As a toddler, not quite two years old, I coughed, gagged, and shivered as Dad pressed my soaking body against his shoulder, his large hands wrapped tightly around me, hugging me as I trembled. Squirming from my father's grasp, I reached out, crying and stretching my hands toward my mother.

"What happened?" Mom said as she turned from the sink and rushed to me, panicked.

"She fell in the pond," Dad said. "I thought Barbara was right beside me. When I saw splashing, I ran to her but my feet tangled and I tripped."

Mom snatched me from his arms and dashed to the bathroom. My drenched overalls streamed water along the oak-planked hallway.

"Dick grabbed her first," my father called to the shadow of Mom's disappearing figure.

"I'm glad she's safe," Dick said as he poked his head into the kitchen. "I've left your pole and tackle box by the back door, Jim. I'm going back to fishing. Let me know if I can help."

My father and Dick Robertson, both in their thirties, had become fast friends since our family moved to Connecticut several months earlier. As next-door neighbors on Leroy Avenue, they often fished in the pond behind the Robertson's stone house. Uncle Dick, as we called him, owned the *Darien Review*, the town's weekly newspaper, and his family often joined us for games and socializing.

Mom knelt on the tile floor and removed my wet, cold clothes. She turned on both spigots of the claw-footed bathtub and sat me in the heating water. Mom bent over the tub's edge, wringing a washcloth above my head. Its cascading warmth flowed across my back and chest and I slowly began to thaw. After she felt I was sufficiently comfortable, she brought me to a standing position and wrapped a soft towel around my body. Our old black Labrador, Leo, stood at attention near the side of the iron bathtub, his gray muzzle protruding toward me, his dark eyes watching the unfolding drama. Even at the age of ten, he was a proud guard dog. My three-year-old sister, Virginia, and I were his charges. But only inside. He was too feeble to follow us around our property.

Mom carried me to the living room and collapsed on the sofa. I snuggled into her soft body while she swayed back and forth, humming soothing sounds and cradling me. She took the colorful, black-bordered afghan she had crocheted years before and tossed it over my shoulders. I sucked my finger and sniffled into Mom's chest.

Dad ditched his rubber galoshes at the back door and walked into the living room, staring at the two of us.

"She's just scared. She was only in the water a few seconds."

"What? She could have drowned. Why weren't you watching her?" Mom scolded. "You know how unpredictable she is."

Looking at my father's muddy jersey, she added, "You should change your shirt, Jim. You're almost as wet as Barbara."

Virginia climbed next to Mom and nestled with me under the afghan. We listened to Mom's warning words.

"Don't ever go near Uncle Dick's pond! It's very dangerous. Look what happened to Barbara," she said. "You two stay under the blanket while I get some dry clothes." She returned with a cotton nightgown, removed my towel, and pulled a pink nightie over my head.

"Now go play while I make dinner," she said as she unwrapped us from the afghan and placed me on the carpet.

Later that evening Virginia and I walked into the room we shared and knelt beside our beds. While Mom and Dad watched, we bowed our heads and folded our hands. I had not yet begun to talk so I mumbled sounds while Virginia recited the nightly prayer.

"Now I lay me down to sleep, I pray the Lord my soul to keep. If I should die before I wake, I pray the Lord my soul to take."

After the prayer we clambered over our colorful bedspreads and slid between the sheets. Mom crossed to the window and lifted the wooden sash a couple of inches. She was a fresh air fanatic and felt we needed to have an open window at night, whether in summer or winter. Mom and Dad kissed us goodnight and stood at our door, watching as the splash of the moon's light caused shadows to dance across the walls.

"Sleep tight and don't let the bedbugs bite," Dad said as he softly shut the door. I heard them walk down the hall and closed my eyes. The down pillow enveloped my head and my bed felt warm. A faint breeze blew through the screened window. My eyelids slipped heavily over my eyes and I fell fast asleep.

# BARBARA'S HAIRCUT

"What did you do?" Mom asked a few months later as she charged into the kitchen, carrying a handful of evergreens from the bushes that edged our backyard. She had planned to decorate the house with silver ribbons and winter foliage.

"She needed a haircut," Virginia said, her hands on her hips looking straight up at Mom. I stood beside my sister, wearing a pink one-piece outfit, with a bewildered look on my face. *Was I in trouble?*

"There's hardly any hair left. You cut it all off," Mom said. "Where're my scissors?"

"In the bathroom."

"You're not to take my scissors. You know that."

"But her hair was too long. I asked Barbara and she said 'okay.'"

"What! She doesn't even talk."

"Well, she sat on the toilet so I guessed it was okay."

Mom reached over and took my hand, shepherding me outside. While I stood in the grass, she brushed stray strands from my shoulders, arms, and back. She looked at the chaos on top of my head and tousled my remaining hair, checking to see if she could mend the damage.

"Wait 'til your father comes home!"

"Don't tell Dad," Virginia wailed, tears filling her eyes, no longer defiant.

"I won't have to say a thing. One look at Barbara and he'll know."

It took several months before my hair began to show enough length to shape into something presentable. Not beautiful, just presentable. In the meantime, the scissors were placed on the top shelf in the medicine cabinet, no longer accessible to an arrogant daughter and her nimble fingers.

# BIRTHDAY PONY

During the following April with patches of melting snow lurking in the shadows of dark tree trunks, many months after my disastrous haircut, our family celebrated Virginia's fourth birthday. I had finally begun to talk although I rarely said much. Virginia was my spokesperson. If anyone asked me a question, she voiced her opinion and answered before I could utter a word.

For the party, Mom had hired an elderly man to transport his pony and cart to our home. Virginia loved horses and had a collection in our shared bedroom, two shelves crowded with ceramic, wooden, and metal toy horses. She begged to have a real horse for her birthday. Instead, she received a cart-pulling pony for the afternoon. Our New York family arrived from Bronxville and joined us for an afternoon of fun-filled festivities.

Once the brown mare and his handler appeared, our three cousins donned warm jackets and joined Virginia and me in a tan-colored, wicker buggy. For an hour or so, the skinny man, dressed in bib overalls, sat on the front bench and commanded his pony to walk up and down our driveway. The rumbling of cart wheels over rough terrain filled the air with pure pleasure. Contagious laughter erupted from the knot of cousins sitting in the back. When he requested the pony to trot, we waved and shouted with joy.

Our parents stood before the garage doors below the side of the house, watching us travel the driveway. Wearing trench coats over dresses and suits, with cocktails and cigarettes in hand, they laughed right along with us. They nestled in a compact semi-circle as the setting sun shined through tree leaves, splashing its rays on diamond rings and broaches.

When it came time for the outdoor festivities to end, Dad thanked the gray-haired man and pressed some extra money into his palm. He walked away and loaded the mare and cart into his trailer. The cousins waved to the man as he struggled to step onto the running board on the side of his truck.

When we could no longer see the trailer, the family moved to the stepping stones near the front door. Warming temperatures encouraged purple pansies and yellow daffodils to bloom next to the house. It was a beautiful but chilly spring day.

We gathered in the cozy living room for snacks and drinks. Virginia opened her gifts while we oohed and aahed at the new games and toy horses. The cousins sat on the carpeted floor and checked out her presents while our parents talked about the high price of meat and nylons. And the seemingly never-ending war in the Orient and Europe. Newspapers covered the conflicts. News from radios flooded the airwaves. U-boats off the New Jersey shore, submarines and torpedoes. Roosevelt and Hitler.

Mom entered the room with a cake and candles and the serious subjects changed. We sang "Happy Birthday" to my smiling sister. Virginia made a wish and blew out five candles, one for each of her four years and one to grow on.

Mom, her dark hair pulled back in a bun, cut the cake and Dad added vanilla ice cream. Soon the party was over. The relatives gathered their coats and piled into shiny, but outmoded, vehicles. We stood outside and waved as their cars puttered up the driveway toward Leroy Avenue. With the government's mandatory wartime speed of 35 miles per hour, the "Victory Speed" as it was called, it'd be well over an hour before they'd be home. By then, Virginia and I would be in bed, sound asleep.

# MAIL PICKUP

"Let's get the mail," Mom said a few weeks later. Our white house sat on a rock ledge, quite a distance from Leroy Avenue. I reached for her hand as we walked out the front door. As an almost three-year-old, it took all my strength to keep up with my mother while we tramped over the dirt driveway. She pointed out birds, wildflowers, and trees on our journey to retrieve the mail. She was an educator at heart and was forever teaching us about nature and its unique beauty. Because Virginia spent each morning at Plumfield School, a private educational facility on Pear Tree Point Road, I was alone with Mom. This was our special time. When we reached the mailbox at Leroy Avenue, Mom pointed to the cows across the street and told me they were chewing their cud.

"What's a cud?"

"They love grass and eat it all day long. Then they lie down and bring the grass back from their stomach and into their mouth so they can chew it again."

I wasn't sure what that meant but it didn't sound good. However, I liked cows and waved to them after we collected the mail and began our stroll back to the house.

"Look at that," Mom said as she pointed to an overhead branch.

Squawking in the nearby tree was a noisy blue jay, rubbing its beak against a moss-covered limb. She told me the mother and father stayed together for life. After another look at the striking blue and white bird, we left the shadows under the tree and walked to the front door.

# COW PASTURE

"Rise and shine," Dad called. The morning light illuminated the dark woods around our house as we climbed out of bed. It was Sunday morning and Mom was still sleeping with our new sister, Mary Gail. She had been born during the holiday season four months earlier. Virginia and I smelled coffee and heard the pot percolating as we sat at our tiny, children's table. Dad fixed us toast, twisted orange halves in a glass juice squeezer, and poured milk in our bowls of Cheerios. While we ate, Dad relaxed in his chair with a cigarette while he enjoyed another cup of coffee. Strong and black.

"My trike won't work. Can you fix it?" Virginia asked.

With a few more pestering comments, Dad agreed to help. They left for the garage underneath our house. I watched them mend the wounded three-wheeler, puttering back and forth in the space below the side of the house. They were intent on their chore and forgot all about me.

*"I'll help, too,"* I thought. *"I'll get the mail."*

Not knowing mail was not delivered on Sunday, I decided to walk to our mailbox. I had made up my mind and trudged to Leroy Avenue, checking the marshy woods bordering our driveway. When I made it to the paved road, I realized I wasn't tall enough to

18

reach the mailbox. However, I did see the familiar cows across the street.

A half dozen brown and white cows stared at me as I walked toward them, inquisitive and unafraid, calling, "Here, Brownie. Here, Brownie."

Crawling under the bottom fence rail, I grabbed some grass and stuck out my hand. All the cows backed up but one. She came to me, her slobbery pink nose stretching out to smell what I held.

Just then a black car slowed and pulled to the side of the road. A dark-haired woman emerged. She silently strolled to the fence, not wanting to scare me or the cows.

"Come here, little girl," she said. "I don't think you should be there."

I walked back to the fence and, once again, crawled under the lowest rail, further smudging my pale pants in the process.

"Let's get you home. Where do you live?"

I pointed across the street and down toward our black mailbox. The lady took my hand and walked me to her car. She opened the passenger side door and lifted me into the seat. Once she turned her car around, drove to our mailbox, and chauffeured me down the driveway to my house, she said, "I don't think your parents know you're not home."

When we arrived, Dad left the garage with Virginia in tow and approached the oncoming vehicle. He was surprised to see me sitting in the front seat. Looking straight up at him, my hands folded neatly in my lap. He helped me out of the car and leaned in the open door. The woman told Dad where she had found me.

"Thank you so much. I really appreciate your stopping."

"I was glad to help."

As the woman drove away, Dad pulled me closer.

"What were you doing?"

"Getting the mail," I said. "You were busy and I wanted to help."

"Who was that?" Mom called a few seconds later from the front door. She carried infant Gail, wrapped in a blanket, next to her chest.

"Oh, some woman just brought Barbara home."

"What do you mean, 'home'?" Mom asked as she walked toward the stone staircase leading to the driveway.

"Barbara decided to pick up the mail. She was trying to help but couldn't reach the box. That's when she saw the cows."

"What? She crossed Leroy?"

"Yes! And she was in the pasture with the cows."

"Thank goodness for that woman! Weren't you watching her?"

"I thought she was inside with you. Virginia and I were in the garage fixing her trike."

"What," Mom whispered in my ear, "am I going to do with you?" She reached for my hand and led me back to the house.

# RATIONS

The following Tuesday morning, Mom placed a glass of freshly squeezed orange juice, some toast, and a bowl of cereal on the kitchen table. After Dad sat for breakfast, he slathered his toast with butter and added milk to his bowl of Grape-Nuts. The sugar container rested in the center, a little spoon leaning on its rim.

"After you leave, I'll cut the butter into four pieces. It'll be easier to handle," Mom said as she removed the yellow block, placing it on a cutting board. "It's too large for the butter dish."

When he drained his coffee, Dad rose from the table. He had a fondness for Brooks Brothers suits and was, as always, stylishly dressed, especially going to his office in New York City. Invariably, a clean white handkerchief peeked from his breast pocket. He walked with Mom to the Crosley, our tiny station wagon parked in the garage. She picked a blue bachelor button from nearby flowers and inserted it into his lapel, kissing him on the cheek. Virginia, Mom, and I waved as he drove out the driveway on his way to the Noroton Heights train station.

When Mom returned to the kitchen with Virginia and me at her side, she saw the cutting board on the floor. No butter was in sight. *What happened?* After checking the floor and inspecting our dog, she surmised that Leo had put his front paws on a chair and pushed his muzzle over the table, knocking everything to the floor. He had eaten the whole block of butter. Mom practically cried at the mess. Old Leo looked up and cocked his head, not knowing why she was so upset. We didn't know either.

As soon as Dad returned that evening, we learned about rationing. Besides meat, sugar, and shoes, the most significant item restricted was butter, especially for my father who had an irresistible passion for that dairy product. Families were allocated one pound of butter each month. And now it was gone. I'm not sure Leo understood his scolding but we certainly did. Butter was a precious item, not to be wasted.

To save for the war effort, the national government instituted scrap drives. Our family collected tin foil, tin cans, rubber bands, and newspapers. We filled a drawer in the kitchen with rolls of string, balls of tin foil, and rubber bands — the rubber and tin foil were destined for the scrap drive and the string for us to reuse. Every month or so, Mom gathered us in her car and drove to Andy's Mobilgas in Noroton Heights to deposit our collected items. After the drop-off, we joined a line of vehicles snaking around the block, a black stamp on our windshield. It signified that our car was used for nonessential travel and was mandated to receive no more than three gallons a week. Some commuters had gone through their gas allotment and had to ride bicycles to the train stations. Farmers and policemen obtained eight-gallon allotments, or red stamps, as they were crucial for the country.

# THE NEW HOUSE

We lived in the leased Leroy house for two years while my parents looked for a permanent home, near to water and with tennis access. They were not typical Darien residents who golfed or sailed but were avid "racket" players, anything from tennis to ping pong to badminton.

They liked Noroton Bay, a private area at the far end of Nearwater Lane, but the realtor voiced his concern, "it occasionally floods." The fifteen acres of Noroton Bay were comprised entirely of landfill, from the cleaning and dredging of Goodwives River in the 1920s.

Eventually, they found a house just to their liking. It was located in Noroton Manor, not far from Nearwater Lane, and close to the new Hindley Elementary School being built and designated to open within a year or two. The realtor informed my parents that Indians named the nearby stream, "Noroton," a stretch of water flowing into Holly Pond and separating Darien from Stamford.

"There's a lot of history here. You'll find stone walls from the 1600s and maybe an arrowhead or two."

The Association bordered Holly Pond, had two clay tennis courts, and many undeveloped lots with plenty of fields. The colonial-style house, built in 1926, stood on the corner of Outlook and Woodland Drives. The price was $25,000 for the three-bedroom, one-and-a-half-bathroom home with an attached two-car garage. In 1946, the average house with no garage cost about $9,000. For us to live in a town with excellent schools, to be near beaches and tennis courts, and to be close to the railroad line to New York City made it the perfect home to buy. We were fortunate our father had the financial means to make the purchase.

# PRESCHOOL
## 1945 - 1947

# OUTLOOK DRIVE

I peeked out the side window of our maroon Chevrolet and saw a two-story, white house with an ivy-covered brick chimney. The house looked huge. But then, I was only three-and-a-half-years old.

We pulled to the garage and Dad stepped out, flicking a still-smoldering cigarette to the ground. A Lucky Strike. He stepped on the butt and turned to open the car's backdoor. It was late afternoon and Mom was tired. She sat in the front seat with six-month-old Gail on her lap. Virginia and I fetched our little leather suitcases from the vehicle's floor and climbed out. Most of our belongings had arrived earlier that morning. Mom had stopped by afterward to make beds and to straighten furniture.

"Your room is at the top of the stairs, Barbara," Dad said. "Virginia, your room is next."

Excitedly, I followed Virginia through the kitchen, dining room, and into the foyer. We both glanced toward the living room before ascending the stairs. Around the curved landing and up two more steps to the hallway and our individual rooms.

I twisted the glass knob and opened my door, standing for a moment, amazed to have a room of my own. Flanking the window on the far wall were two single beds with a cast iron radiator in the middle. A blossoming plum tree, all thick and pink, appeared outside the window. I pulled out a drawer of the mahogany dresser and emptied my suitcase.

Mom placed Gail in an old-fashioned cradle in the dressing room next to the master bedroom and then took Virginia and me on a tour of the house. The dining room not only had a mahogany table with eight chairs but also a triangular corner cabinet, all antique gifts from Mom's mother. On the floor by the front wall sat boxes of china and crystal, waiting to be put away.

From there we walked through French doors into a flagstone-floored screened porch already furnished with a gliding sofa and two matching padded chairs.

In the kitchen all the cabinets and appliances had been built-in. Boxes rested on laminate countertops. Bowls, plates, and glasses. We even had a washing machine for clothes, our first one without a wringer.

We next inspected a sparsely decorated living room. A blue-gray loveseat, an upholstered chair with white doilies on its back and arms, a brass floor lamp, and a smoking stand — an ashtray on a pedestal — were all that occupied the room. A fireplace and two built-in bookcases dominated one end of the room. Cardboard boxes stood open on the floor, filled with books ready to stock the nearby shelves.

Continuing into the sunroom, we saw it was almost empty except for an upright piano. Ten windows along three walls allowed the sun to shine into the room all day long.

From the foyer we strolled along a corridor to another set of French doors which led to the small back porch. In the narrow hallway Mom had placed a small table and two straight-backed chairs. Our one telephone rested on its top. Underneath the stairs, a small bathroom concealed a toilet and a corner sink.

When it was time for dinner that first night, I sat on top of two thick books in the dining room while Gail was cushioned in a highchair. Even at this young age, we all ate our evening meal in the dining room and listened to Mom and Dad, their thoughts and opinions. Eventually, we also contributed. With our own feelings, our own beliefs, and our own attitudes. But not yet.

# LUCKY, THE FAMILY DOG

Within a month of our arrival at our new home, we acquired a beagle puppy. Old Leo had died at our place on Leroy. My parents ordered a new puppy from Pennsylvania. He was to arrive in Darien by train. Along the way to the transfer at a New York station, the train collided with a truck but the puppy survived. We named him, "Lucky."

Winter was ending and spring beckoned the following week. Mom asked Virginia and me to come to the kitchen. She ushered us to a corner and asked us to stand by the door leading to the basement. Lucky sat beside us and looked at her. *What was she doing?*

"Stand up straight," she instructed.

Mom leaned Virginia against the door jamb. On the wall next to the stairs hung cleaning supplies: a broom, mop, and Mom's apron. Using a pencil, she drew a horizontal stripe on the wooden frame across Virginia's head, at the highest point.

"Okay. You're next, Barbara."

Our names and dates were added to the pencil lines. Each year Mom lined us against the door and made new marks. This was an annual ritual, to measure how much we had grown.

While Mom decorated, Dad installed "snow guards" in each bedroom. These five-inch-high glass panes stretched across the bottom window sills, angling into each bedroom. Even in winter, Mom opened our windows. With snow guards, no icy flakes escaped into the house, just clean cold air.

As the house developed, Virginia took white chalk from the kitchen junk drawer and had drawn an eight-square outline on the road for hopscotch. Using a flat rock, Virginia and I jumped the squares. The Austin twins, Mimi and Betsy, saw us and came over to play. Within a month of moving to our new home, Virginia and I knew all the children on our two streets. They came to play hopscotch and to meet the newcomers.

# VICTORY GARDENS

Virginia and I helped our parents plant a Victory Garden in our backyard. These gardens were introduced to Americans so the produce from farmers could go overseas for our fighting troops, not to be consumed by local residents. Victory Gardens reduced the vegetable demand at grocery stores during the war, and although the government's promotion of Victory Gardens ended with the war, a renaissance movement sprouted in support of self-sufficiency and eating seasonally to improve health, all of which my mother strongly supported.

In many ways, Mom was before her time. She placed marigolds around the perimeter to keep snails and bugs from invading our garden. It was nature's way of discouraging them without the use of pesticides. She was very smart, having skipped two grades and graduated from high school at sixteen. She loved to question and explore, to learn and discover. She encouraged us to do the same.

Our next-door neighbors came over while we worked outside and introduced themselves. We became close to the family and called Mr. and Mrs. Corbett, "Uncle Jim" and "Auntie Dot." Once they saw our personal Victory Garden, they suggested we band together and make a large one in the field across Woodland Drive.

Using shovels and hoes, our parents and neighbors cleared the land of tall grasses and loosened the soil.

The adults wrapped tomato branches on wooden sticks and sowed rows of corn, string beans, radishes, peppers, carrots, and lettuce. Children knelt in the dirt and pulled weeds. Lucky dug holes.

Getting ready for bed that evening, exhausted from weeding and working as a "gofer" around the Victory Garden, I noticed Mom had placed pink roses in a vase on my dresser. Pink-flowered wallpaper covered my bedroom walls. Green vines connected one pink rose to another. Lying in bed later that night, I traced them with my fingers, back and forth, up and down. For a young girl who loved pink colors, this was heaven.

# TRADESMEN

As the weeks progressed, our family received routine calls from local tradesmen. They were a welcome addition and supplied numerous items, assisting my mother with her daily chores.

The milkman in his white uniform came twice a week. He carried a wire container filled with glass bottles and left fresh milk in a metal box outside, between our garage doors. He removed the empty glass bottles and returned them to his truck to be cleaned at the factory and to be reused over and over again.

The mailman stopped by daily, hefting a leather pouch stuffed with mail and wearing a light blue uniform. He periodically enjoyed a cup of coffee with Mom before continuing with his route.

A man with newspapers dropped off paper editions twice a day, morning and evening, throwing them onto our driveway.

The trashmen arrived weekly, picking up our two metal bins, throwing the garbage into a truck and replacing the empty containers next to our slanted cellar doors.

The fishman came by every Friday. He was short and squat with a thick mustache. There were many Catholics living in Darien and in their interpretation of the Bible, they were not allowed to eat meat on Friday.

Alice, a heavyset colored woman in her early thirties, arrived to clean our house every Tuesday. She rode a bus from Stamford to the corner of Outlook Drive and the Boston Post Road and walked the block to our house. Alice helped Mom with ironing and then dusted and vacuumed until our house sparkled. When it was time for a midday meal, Alice ate in the kitchen while Mom lunched at the table in the dining room.

The most important of all these tradesmen was the Good Humor man. Almost daily during the summer, we heard bells chime along the road and screamed for Mom.

"It's the Good Humor man," we yelled. "Hurry! Hurry!"

Mom pulled out coins buried in her apron pocket while Virginia and I circled her with our hands extended. She gave each of us a nickel and we ran from the kitchen. Standing in line at the back of the gleaming white, refrigerated truck, we waited impatiently. Finally, it was my turn. I chose chocolate ice cream in a sugar cone, my favorite.

# THE STUMP DISCOVERED

Two of the Johnston siblings, Jane, a year older than Virginia, and Robbie, my age, came to our house and asked us if we would like to see "The Stump." Of course, we would. Out the door we went and into a world of make-believe. We traipsed across the street, up Mrs. Lewis' driveway, through her backyard, over a stone wall, and into the woods. For Virginia and me, this was unfamiliar territory. We hadn't ventured past our house and the bordering two streets since we had arrived at our new house a few months earlier. When we reached the stump, I thought it was gigantic. The base was over six feet in diameter and stood at least a dozen feet high.

"Follow me," Jane said as she crawled into a tree hollow, what we thought was an owl's hole, and climbed straight up inside the stump. Robbie followed and, in a few seconds, they were waving to us, high on a broken-off limb. We did as Jane suggested and squeezed through the hole, my shoulders scraping its edges. When we reached the top, they had already taken places on different limb remnants, each one branching out from the large base. We joined them and sat on our own limbs, towering above the ground, all of us in dungarees and tee shirts.

"Well, what'd you think?" Jane asked.

"Great," Virginia said. "How'd you find it?"

"It's not far from our backyard. We're always in the woods. Wait 'til you see the other things we've found."

The stump became one of our favorite places to play. It was so large, the tree probably began growing during the Revolutionary War. From that day on, we stayed outside and didn't bother to come home unless we were hungry, hurt, or our house bell rang. If Virginia and I didn't hear the ringing bell, Lucky did. All the neighbors' homes had house bells. We each knew our family's particular sound and so did the dogs.

A month or so later, Robbie and I met at the stump. He had found some cigarette butts and wanted to show me how to smoke. We were both four years old when we took a shortened cigarette and put it between our lips. We pretended to blow out plumes of smoke and flicked imaginary ashes into the air.

"Next time, I'll bring some matches. We'll try this for real," Robbie said.

At our next meeting at the stump, he had a bunch of wooden matches in a small red box. We crawled through the hole and sat close together on a sturdy limb.

"Lean forward," he said after handing me a butt. I put the cigarette remains between my lips and bent toward him. He struck a match on the side strip and put it to the white paper.

"Puff," he said.

I tried but nothing happened. Then I watched him light a cigarette and begin to inhale. The ash at the end of the butt glowed. Wow! This was great. I started to puff and saw my cigarette flare. And so, we sat, pretending to be grown-ups. Two little kids, high in the stump, puffing away on our cigarette butts.

Robbie and I became inseparable and the stump became our meeting place. We clambered through the hollow and sat on limbs, facing each other. Rarely smoking now unless it was with candy cigarettes, but most of the time, we just told family stories or exchanged ideas of fun things to do.

"Are you going to put cards in your spokes? I asked, thinking of his blue bike.

"Of course. I'm going to ride in the parade."

"I might ride, too. The cards sound super. I'm adding some red ribbons to my handlebars. And I'll ring my bell."

⎯⎯⎯⎯⎯⎯

On another adventure at the stump, Mimi and Betsy joined Robbie and me in the woods. Robbie had brought a bundle of crab grass. Squishing a wide blade between his thumbs, he blew into the crevice and a piercing sound emerged. *How neat is this?* He gave each of us a blade and showed us what to do. Before long, we had the woods alive with screeches. Reverberating screams pierced the air. No bird or any other creature dared come near us. Only patient Lucky and Robbie's Dalmatian, Spot, sat at the base of the stump. They would not leave us, no matter what noises emerged.

Eventually, the woods beckoned and we walked to a drainage creek at the bottom of a hill. There in one of the pools, we saw a cluster of tadpoles, swimming sporadically under an overhang. Betsy knelt and cupped the baby frogs, their inch-long bodies wriggled in her palms. She showed them to Lucky and Spot, curiously watching the polliwogs swirl and struggle. When she let the tadpoles go, they swam under a branch and disappeared. The dogs stared into the creek and stuck their noses into nearby grasses. The tadpoles had vanished.

Soon the sun began to fade. Light filtered through leaves and a slight wind caressed the trees. I heard my house bell. Lucky's ears pricked up. It was time to go.

When I arrived in the kitchen, I watched Mom preparing a drink for Dad. Most of the neighboring adults had alcoholic drinks before dinner. It was a ritual that consumed the area.

She opened the refrigerator door and lifted a metal door's latch to the freezer compartment. Stuffed inside were two ice cube trays; that's all it could hold. She removed one and pulled the handle, releasing the ice from the tray. Taking a few cubes, she placed them in the metal grinder above the sink.

"Can I do it?" I asked.

Mom wrapped her arms around me and lifted me above the sink. Sitting on the porcelain edge with my feet in the basin, I turned the handle. Mom held her hand on the top of the device so ice couldn't escape and placed a goblet below. I heard crushing ice falling into the glass.

"That's enough," she said and lifted me from the sink. Instead of liquor, she added tomato juice and a celery stalk. Once she put the drink on a tray and added a few crackers and cheese, she walked to the living room. Lucky and I followed.

Dad sat in his favorite lounge chair, smoking a cigarette and reading the evening paper.

"Well, what have we here? Mom, Barbara, and Lucky. What could be better?" Dad said as he put his newspaper to the side and smiled at us. Mom placed the tray on top of his side table and returned to the kitchen.

# PAN SLEDDING

During our first winter at Outlook Drive, the sun had barely cleared the treetops before slipping away under dense, dark clouds. Snowflakes fell in large clumps, a few at a time. Then in a mass, over and over, until it stayed locked on our lawn. Virginia and I peered out the back porch's window, watching Dad shovel the driveway.

"Here, take these," Mom said.

She handed me a metal pie pan and gave Virginia a circular brass plate. Mom had bundled us in nylon bib pants with matching jackets and knitted mittens. Each mitten was connected by a thick strand of yarn, threaded through the sleeves and across our backs. We couldn't lose them. They were tied to each other. With pans in our hands, we stood outside next to Dad as he continued to scrape snow from the porch to the garage.

"Here. Take my hand," Dad said as he put down the shovel and reached out to Virginia. "Don't worry. I'll hold you."

I watched as he supported her. She walked up the slanted edge of the cellar door and cautiously moved to the center. Carefully placing her bottom on the brass plate, she sat and lifted her feet. Down she went, sliding along the slope of the door and flying out onto the packed driveway.

"That's fun," Virginia said, her hands in the air. "Can I do it again?"

"Let Barbara try it next."

Dad took my mittened hand and braced me as I climbed up the side of the cellar door. Not even slowing, I shuffled to the center, placed the pie pan below my fanny and sat. Once I raised my feet, I zoomed down the slope, careening out onto the driveway.

"You're on your own now," Dad said. "I have to finish shoveling. The mailman will be here shortly. He'll need a path to our door."

For the next hour, we took turns climbing the side of the cellar door and sliding to the bottom. Mom came out with her Kodak Brownie camera and took pictures of the two of us, huge smiles on our faces, holding the metal pans, standing in front of our new-found slide.

From the radio in the kitchen, we heard "White Christmas" by Bing Crosby. The song cast sounds to the outside while Mom and Dad watched us go up and down the cellar door. With their encouragement, we trudged to the snow-covered lawn and dropped to our knees. Rolling onto our backs, we spread our arms and legs, moving them back and forth. Snow angels! More photos for Mom to take.

# SPANKINGS

"Wait till your father comes home," Mom warned me that following spring.

Knowing I was going to be spanked, I cried and begged forgiveness. Virginia heard my sobs and whispered, "Don't worry. I'll help."

As soon as Dad's car appeared in our driveway, I ran to her room. She took a hard-bound, Little Golden book and placed it in the back of my underpants. Dad climbed the stairs and approached me with a stern look.

"Why did you disobey Mom?" he asked, staring down at me.

"I don't know," I said, looking at my bare feet.

"Come with me," he said as he took my little hand and led me to the bathroom, clothed in underpants and a tee-shirt. I knew the routine. Dad sat on the toilet lid and lectured me about following Mom's orders. Face to face. He turned me around and leaned me over the rim of the tub. He took two swats at my butt, making sure I understood the severity of my misdemeanor. As an adult, I know he saw the book, but as a little four-year-old, I thought it would protect me. In reality, the book reverberated against my bottom and left deep, red impressions.

"I hope you've learned your lesson. When your Mom asks you to do something, do it!"

He led me from the bathroom and I immediately ran to my bedroom, tears streaming down my cheeks. After Dad had disappeared in the living room, Virginia sneaked into my room.

"See, it wasn't so bad. I knew the book would help."

"I hate the book. It made it worse!" I pouted while sitting on the edge of my bed. Virginia sat beside me, trying to console me.

"Come on. Let's go to my room. We can play with my horses 'til dinner."

# NOROTON BAY BEACH CLUB

The first month we lived in the Leroy house, my parents joined the Noroton Bay Beach Club. By the time we moved to Outlook Drive, we were regulars. Whenever the sun shone and the temperature reached skyward, Mom gathered us in the car and drove to the beach. Mothers and children descended on the shore, laden with beach chairs, sand buckets, and mini shovels. Mom brought a playpen for Gail and draped a cloth over the top railings to offer shade. As Gail slept, Mom taught me how to swim. Virginia dog paddled near shore while Mom held me afloat. Kicking and stroking. Then she let go. I was off, paddling right beside Virginia.

"My little mermaids," Mom cheered, standing near us, the tide lapping at the sand. She dropped lower in the water and began to sidestroke, making sure her head stayed above the water, keeping her hair dry. The three of us swam about twenty yards and then I stood.

"Now, can I swim off the pier?" I asked.

"Absolutely not." Mom said. "When you can swim for thirty minutes without a break, then you can go to the pier."

"Why can't I go now? I can swim just like Virginia."

"No, you can't. I'll keep watch. You'll be able to swim from the pier before long," Mom said. "For now, just enjoy the water."

We swam along the shoreline until it was time for lunch. When we reached our towels, we found Gail sitting on a padded mattress, playing with wooden blocks underneath the cloth canopy.

Mom had us sit on towels, facing the water. She passed sandwiches, apple slices, and cookies. After lunch, we took the mandatory thirty-minute nap before heading to the water.

"You don't want to get a cramp," Mom said. "That's why we need to rest after eating."

Following an hour of swimming, Mom carried Gail and walked Virginia and me toward rocks protruding from a spit of land near Weed Beach. Fiddler crabs ran into their holes as we strolled over the sand. Seagulls flew past in slashes of white across the crystal-clear sky, black tips on their wings. Squawking and screeching. Soaring and sweeping.

As Virginia and I sat quietly on rocks at the far end of Noroton Bay, our feet in tidal pools, marine life burst into view. Minnows and snails moved around the edges as we stared into the captive water, waves periodically splashing over the pool's edge.

"Look at this," I said pointing to a crab moving over a nearby rock, away from the tidal pool.

"It's a hermit crab," Mom said. "See that shell? He took it for his house. As he grows, he changes his house and finds a bigger shell."

"How long does it live?" Virginia asked.

"Twenty years, maybe longer."

"Look at this stone. See how flat it is," Virginia said as water lapped at her toes. "Watch me."

She bent to the side and tossed the stone out into the bay. It bounced over and across the waves three times before disappearing. She picked another stone and did it again. We watched it splashing as it skipped across the surface.

"Here. You try," she said as she handed me a flat, gray stone. It lay warm in my open hand and I rotated it into position.

My first throw was a dud, falling immediately from view. With a better twist of my wrist, I managed to skim a stone several times. Now it was a contest. Who could skip a stone the most times? Even Mom joined the challenge. Gail sat on the water's edge, splashing and giggling. For the next few minutes, we skipped stones. Mom, being an excellent tennis player, twisted her wrist and outdid Virginia and me. She was the champ.

# BEFORE INOCULATIONS

One of Mom's idiosyncrasies was for me to play with nearby children when they developed measles, mumps, or chickenpox. As there were no vaccines for these infections, she wanted me to be exposed and to contract the illnesses before going to kindergarten.

"Susan has the chickenpox," Mom said, smiling with delight one day. "I'll call Mrs. Fedlar and see if you can go over and play. You can bring a coloring book. Susan'll like that."

The following week, I began to feel sick. Mom relegated me to the couch in the sunroom with Lucky on the floor beside me. She returned with a thermometer.

"Stick it under your tongue and close your mouth. I'll check it in two minutes."

While waiting for the required minutes to pass, Lucky came close to me, wagging his tail. My skin unveiled a mass of sores, and I didn't have much of an appetite. Meals in the sunroom consisted of chicken noodle soup, ginger ale, and Saltine crackers. Reading books and coloring helped while away my period of sickness.

Mom's routine was not much different for colds. I had to gargle with warm salty water, standing on a stool in the kitchen, facing the sink with my head bent backward. I slept in the sunroom, its abundant rays warming and welcoming me, flooding the room with sunshine all day long. Mom would perch on the edge of the couch and rub my chest with Vick's VapoRub — a greasy, camphor-smelling ointment. Whenever a shiver overtook me, Mom placed a cold washcloth on my forehead while a hot towel soothed my chest. After a few days, I began to feel better, to go outside and play.

"But not yet," Mom cautioned. "Look what I have." She held a colorfully wrapped present and handed it to me.

"Don't tear the paper."

*Of course not.* I carefully undid the ribbon and paper, all to be placed in the attic, all to be reused. I opened the lid of the box and looked at a black contraption.

"What is it?"

"It's a View-Master. I'll show you how it works," Mom said as she took a round reel and placed it in a slot. "Now, look through the eyepieces."

"Wow. Thanks, Mom," I said as I pushed the lever and watched picture after picture come before my eyes. All in color and all three dimensional.

"Thanks, Mom. Wow! It's almost like my birthday."

# COOKING AND CLOCKS

When Virginia started kindergarten, she attended the original Hindley School on the Boston Post Road, a three-story wooden structure built in 1908. Lucky and I sometimes followed her as it was only three hours of lessons and the teacher didn't mind if I joined the class. I wore dungarees and a tee shirt and most of the other children did likewise. Dresses were for church and parties, not for school. Dungarees helped protect against hurts and occasional bleeding if one fell while playing on the sharp cinder gravel behind the school.

I sat with Lucky on a hinged, locker seat at the back of the classroom and watched the teacher draw pictures and letters. Underneath tall, multi-paned windows, we huddled together. We didn't make any noise as we sat as quietly as possible, listening to books being read.

One day when Virginia and I returned from Hindley, the house was empty. Mom had taken Gail to complete her twice-weekly grocery shopping. Virginia knew Lucky was fed from a can of dogfood and decided she'd make a snack for me. Standing on a stool, she opened the tin of horsemeat and poured the contents into a saucepan. Lucky, his head arched upward, studied her every move, hoping something would drop to the floor. I set the kitchen table with napkins, spoons, and bowls while Virginia stirred the pot. Once the contents were heated, she stepped from the stool and placed a large spoonful into my bowl and stood back to watch. I politely sat and placed a napkin in my lap. I picked up my spoon and took a bite. It tasted terribly.

Just then, Mom walked in with a bag of groceries in one arm and Gail in the other. Carrot greens and a loaf of bread protruded from her paper sack.

"What're you doing?"

"I made her lunch, "Virginia said. "We just got home from school."

"That's dogfood. And you shouldn't be cooking if I'm not home. That's dangerous. Your Dad is going to hear about this," Mom said as she placed Gail in her highchair and grabbed Virginia's hand and marched her upstairs. I heard the bedroom door slam and Mom's footsteps coming downstairs.

"I'll make you a sandwich, Barbara. Then you can go out and play. Virginia will spend the afternoon in her room."

––––––––––––

After lunch, I bolted for the Corbett's house. Auntie Dot opened the kitchen door and beckoned for me to come in.

"Is Uncle Jim home?" I asked.

"He's upstairs in the attic. Go join him. He loves it when you visit."

I scooted through the dining room, past the grandfather clock in the foyer, the grandmother clock on the landing, and up the staircase. I opened the attic door and climbed the last flight of stairs.

"Hi, Uncle Jim. What're you doin'?"

"I found a clock with wooden works," Uncle Jim said. "There's no metal inside. All the gears are carved out of wood. Come see."

I bent over his arm as he opened the back panel of a large mantel clock. Peering into the space, I saw knobs and gears, etched into wood. He took a small brush and swept the inside. With a flashlight shining into the cavity, he took a metal tool and turned the wheels. I watched the brass pendulum swing back and forth. Tick tock. Tick tock.

Antique clocks were Uncle Jim's passion. At the top of the hour, clocks throughout the house began to chime. In the attic with maybe thirty clocks on shelves throughout the space, it sounded like a circus calliope. There were clocks in all sorts of disrepair, one without a glass on its face, another without a pendulum, and some just needed cleaning. Uncle Jim had eight-day clocks and thirty-hour clocks. That meant he was winding some clock every week and others every day. I watched him work, fascinated by his elaborate collection. Visiting Uncle Jim in his attic was the beginning of my love for antique clocks. He liked my enthusiasm and curiosity and told me stories about Connecticut clocks and their makers.

# PLUMFIELD

Before kindergarten, I attended Plumfield, a private school between Pear Tree Point and Long Neck Point Roads. The name Plumfield came from the novel, *Little Women*, and it was started by Mary Rose Hilton in 1931.

One of the first things we learned was the Pledge of Allegiance. Many of the words were hard to pronounce and I didn't know their meanings, but I repeated the pledge in a cadence along with other children. We stood facing an American flag and said the Pledge first thing every morning, our right hands over our hearts.

Afterward, our teacher, Miss Banks, young and pretty, sat in the center of the room and asked us to assemble in a semi-circle on the floor in front of her. She sat on a straight-backed chair, crossed her legs, and read stories to us, nursery rhymes about Jack and Jill who went up the hill, Little Miss Muffet and her spider, and Humpty Dumpty and all the king's men. She taught us to clap and roll our hands to *pat-a-cake, pat-a-cake, baker's man*, to sing the "A, B, C" song, and to count on our fingers. We sang songs, drew pictures, and identified images of farm animals, imitating their sounds.

To the delight of her students, Blackberry, one of the two horses on the property, surprised us whenever he peeked his head into the classroom window. We screamed with joy as he raised and lowered his head, folding his upper lip backward, and neighing as if to say "Hello."

During sun-filled recesses, we ran outside, jumping and running around with our new found friends. We played in a sandbox, swayed on swing sets, and climbed the miniature train built by Mrs. Hilton's son, Ted, when he was in high school. The top of the wooden engine, red and black, stood well above my head. It was followed by yellow or green passenger cars, a blue freight car, and a red caboose.

When walking to the colorful train, the children were often followed by Dinner Kettle, another horse, brown in color with a bell around his neck. He roamed the property with no restraints and loved to follow anyone, hoping for a treat. Plumfield was a child's dream come true.

# HINDLEY ELEMENTARY
## 1947 – 1954

# KINDERGARTEN

The town completed the new Hindley Elementary School in August 1947, an impressive two-story, elongated structure on the corner of Nearwater Lane and the Boston Post Road. A stone wall bordered two sides of the property where battles were fought during the Revolutionary War. The old Hindley School became the "Annex" and was used by sixth graders.

As a five-year-old, I walked with Virginia to the new school, the day after the Labor Day weekend. Before long there was a crowd of youngsters walking on Woodland Drive. Three dogs joined the group. Lucky and Spot along with Johnny Monroe's dog, Dingo. The Austin siblings marched alongside us. A few older students rode their bikes and easily passed our group on the way to school.

My kindergarten teacher, Mrs. Milano, ordered us to hang our jackets on the hooks by the main door and to take a seat, "any seat, don't be picky." I looked at her, frightened by her scowl. She had dark, mousy hair with a touch of gray at her temples. She was slightly plump and short. In a belligerent torrent, she established her class rules.

"Raise your hand and say, "Here," when I call your name."

From a paper attached to a clipboard, she recited, "Danny Abercrombie, Evin Brouard, Everett Card, Kathy

Clemens, Barbara DeForest, Bobby DiChiara, Babby Draper, Janet Franklin, Robbie Johnston, Sandy Leng, Mary McElrath, Johnny Monroe, Barbara Phelps, Dicky Pitts, Robbie Rand, Dave Roberts, Carolyn Sawyer, Alison White, and Mary Sue Young."

"You must also raise your hand if you want to use the bathroom." She paused, "Now does anyone want to go to the bathroom?"

I looked around the room. No one raised their hand. No one moved. She had intimidated us.

"Okay, everyone. Stand and face the flag."

I heard scraping of chairs as we did what she asked.

"Watch me. Place your hand over your heart. Just like this. Now I'll teach you the Pledge of Allegiance. Repeat after me."

"I pledge allegiance to the flag."

"I pledge allegiance to the flag," we repeated. And so, it continued until the last line was said. I recognized the pledge from reciting it at Plumfield but I still didn't know what many of the words meant. With every day's deliverance, her students eventually memorized the pledge and I learned some of the meanings.

"Now we're going to sing the national anthem," she instructed. She tugged a round object, a chromatic pitch instrument, from her pocket and placed it in her mouth. After she produced a note, she repeated the sound with her mouth, singing, "O!" She lifted her free hand to encourage us to sing the sound. Then she sang the first line and paused.

"O! Say can you see, by the dawn's early light."

Finally, we made it through the national anthem and Mrs. Milano told us to take our seats. She walked around the class, her hands on her hips. When she stated my name, I felt her attention on me like a spotlight.

"Stand up and tell me your telephone number," she instructed.

"5-0651," I answered as I stood and looked into her stern face.

"Good, Barbara," she said. "You answered correctly." Smiling, my eyes glistened as I basked in her moment of praise until she asked the next question. "And what is your address?"

I bowed my head, staring at the top of my desk. "I don't know."

"Someday you might get lost or a stranger might take you," she said sternly. "You have to know your telephone number and address."

From that day on she quizzed each of us until we could easily recite our telephone number and home address.

After that first day of school until June, Mrs. Milano frightened me. She paced the room, her hands locked behind her back, and seemed to struggle with the rowdiness of boys. If one acted up, she would grab his arm and drag him to the hall. We heard screams coming through the glass window as she spanked him. We huddled close to our desks, hoping not to be chosen for the next hallway outing.

Mrs. Milano returned to the classroom and stalked the rows in her blocky, brown shoes. Finally, we relaxed when it was "reading" period. We fidgeted, happy in anticipation. *Jack and the Beanstalk, Little Red Riding Hood, Goldilocks and the Three Bears.* The best day in her classroom was when she taught us "Itsy Bitsy Spider" with all the hand signs. We giggled and asked her to do it again, and again. She obliged us and then went back to her demanding routines.

———

During one of the fifteen-minute recesses, we played on the black tarmac outside. The see-saw, swings, hopscotch, a slide, and jump ropes were our choices. Barbara DeForest, the tallest girl in our class and one of my best friends, chose the see-saw. On the narrow board, she sat at one end and I at the other. As I rose, Barbara dropped. We pushed with our legs, going up and down, up and down, until Mrs. Milano blew a whistle. It was time to return to the classroom. Without thinking, I jumped off while Barbara was still high in the air. She crashed to the ground. My end of the board struck me with such speed, my head flew back and blood gushed from a gash on my chin. Blood was everywhere, on my face, over my clothes, dripping into my sneakers.

Mrs. Milano ushered me into the bathroom. Taking some toilet paper, she applied a wad to my face.

"Go tell the nurse," she instructed Barbara, my see-saw companion.

Soon, a nurse appeared and escorted me to her office. I held a paper towel over the wound as we walked up the hallway. She called my mother and had me lie on a couch near her desk. Mom arrived shortly and noticed my chin was still bleeding. The nurse suggested I see a doctor.

"Oh, she'll be all right," Mom replied, still inspecting my wound.

"I don't think so. She'll need stitches. Who should I call?"

"If you really think it's necessary, phone Dr. Ross. Tell him I'll be there in a few minutes."

It's not that Mom didn't like doctors, she just thought most health issues could be handled at home. With obvious reluctance, she helped me from the couch.

"Barbara, tilt your head back. I want to see the cut," Dr. Ross said when we arrived in his examining room. After applying some antiseptic and a numbing lotion, he stitched the cut. Three stitches across the point of my chin. Then a Band-Aid to keep the area clean.

"Give her an aspirin and have her lie down when you get home," he said. "That will let the stitches take hold. She'll be fine tomorrow."

Mom did as he requested. Characteristically, that one day in Dr. Ross's office was the only time in my life she took me to a doctor. It was the same for my sisters. Dad became the one who drove us to medical facilities but not unless it was absolutely necessary.

# CHRISTMAS PREPARATIONS

In December of that year, Mom gathered Virginia, Gail, and me in the living room to make holiday decorations. While Dad secured our Christmas tree in the front corner of the living room, Mom cut long bands of red and green construction paper. She showed Virginia and me how to loop the colorful strips and glue the pieces with rubber cement. Before long, we had a twenty-foot chain. Mom then demonstrated how to string popcorn with upholstery thread and a big-eyed needle. We punctured each kernel and strung one popped corn to another. Two-year-old Gail sat beside us, eating any white substance that broke in the process.

"After Christmas Dad will carry the tree to the field. With popcorn still on it, birds will have their own little party," Mom said. "I'll even spread some bacon fat over a few branches."

During our decorating day, Dad hung bright lights on the tree and Mom arranged strings of beads she had bought as a teenage student in Europe; tiny glass beads of red, gold, blue, and green. Next came strings of popcorn and the red and green chain, then some colorful ornaments. Tinsel, two-foot-long silver strands, were draped precisely over each branch. We stood back and admired our handiwork. The tree looked beautiful. Time for guests to arrive.

"Merry Christmas," Dad said as he welcomed the Robertson family. In walked Aunt Marty, Uncle Dick, and their two children, Polly and Wade. After stowing their coats in the hall closet, Dad took drink orders and Mom showed off our decorations.

Knowing Uncle Dick believed that children should be seen and not heard, Virginia retrieved a deck of cards. While the parents visited at one end of the living room, we sat on the carpet, close to the Christmas tree and played Old Maid. In the background we heard holiday music coming from the Philco record player in the dining room. Record after record tumbled down the center spindle onto the turntable. Dad rose to refill cocktails while Mom passed celery stuffed with whipped peanut butter and ketchup. Another plate had her famous deviled eggs sprinkled with paprika and horseradish.

"Hey, Jim. You forgot the star at the top of the tree," Uncle Dick said.

"So, I did. Where's the star, Florence?"

"It's in the kitchen. I forgot it," Mom said. "Wait here. I'll get it."

When she returned, she brought not only the gold ornament but our old wooden step stool. All the children stood and moved to the side while my father took another sip of bourbon. He handed his glass to Mom, which she exchanged for the large tree topper, a gilded star.

As Dad stepped on the stool, it shuddered slightly, but he ignored its complaint. He moved to the top rung and leaned toward the tree. Suddenly, the stool collapsed, splaying wood pieces over our carpet. Dad crashed into the Christmas tree, still holding the star high above his head.

Uncle Dick tore from his chair to pull Dad from the tree while Aunt Marty burst into laughter. When Dad stood, he brushed needles and tinsel from his clothes while the rest of us howled hysterically.

"When they sing "Joy to the World," I'm sure they didn't mean falling into the Christmas tree," Dad said, laughing alongside us.

The two men bent the uppermost part of the tree, placed the star on top, and returned the tree to its original position. A few ornaments had fallen, parts of the paper chain were crushed, but nothing had broken.

"It looks pretty good, Jim, especially with the star on top," Uncle Dick declared as he stepped back to inspect the decorating. He paused and said, "We're stopping by the grocery store on our way home. Speaking of which, we better get going."

# CHRISTMAS EVE

Five days later on Christmas Eve, we gathered in the living room, sitting cozy and warm, listening to holiday records. We were allowed to open one present each, one present only. It was our family ritual. Dad reached under the Christmas tree and handed Virginia a package and then pulled out another box and offered it to me. The two of us sat on the living room couch and opened our one gift. First Virginia, then me. I received a pink nightgown, Virginia had one in pale green.

Gail cuddled next to Mom on an upholstered chair. She had been fighting a cold and preferred to nuzzle close to Mom. She undid her package with Mom's assistance, untying the ribbon and carefully removing colorful wrapping paper. There inside the box, surrounded by white tissue paper, was a blue nightgown with elaborate stitching sewed diagonally across the top. Mom pulled the nightie over Gail's head and fished an embroidered handkerchief from her sweater's sleeve. She wiped Gail's dripping nose and carried her to the couch.

Virginia and I put on our new nightclothes while Dad moved from his chair to the couch. We sat on both sides of him and Gail snuggled in his lap, holding Mom's hankie. While he read, *'Twas the Night Before Christmas*, Mom gathered papers, bows, and boxes that she would add to the packaging collection in the attic, to be reused over and over again.

After the story we climbed upstairs to our bedrooms. With kisses and wishes for a good night's sleep, Mom walked to my window and raised the sash a half inch. Even with a slight wind blowing outside, I had fresh air flowing into my room, the snow guard holding back any possible ice or flakes of snow. I slid between the flannel sheets and pulled the satin hems of my two blankets to my chin. The smell of mothballs lingered from summer storage but nothing bothered me. Sleep fell over me like a shadow, and I was soon dreaming of presents, of toys and games.

# CHRISTMAS BLIZZARD

Polar air silently swept in from the Atlantic, blasting New England in 1947 with a surprise Christmas snowstorm. A blizzard that buried Darien under two feet of snow. The rising sun transformed the horizon from subtle pink to a dark gray. Large cumulus clouds jostled against each other and rolled across the darkening sky. Storm clouds gathered and snowflakes began to fall in earnest, harder and faster.

"Wake up, Barbara. Let's see what Santa brought."

It was early Christmas morning when Virginia slipped into my room. She leaned over my sleeping body and pulled back the wool blankets. I ignored her and turned to face the wall. I heard pounding against my window. Trees pivoted in the wind and cracked from the cold, knocking against the side of our house.

"Get up. You can't sleep now. It's Christmas!"

Wiping sleep from my eyes, I looked at her. It was still dark outside and freezing air blew from the snow guard, causing me to burrow back under the covers. I hauled the blankets over my head and nestled lower in the bed.

"Come on! Santa's here!"

I reluctantly crawled from my bed and joined Virginia on the landing. We sneaked halfway down the stairs, stopping to crouch, peeking between the white spindles, waiting to see if Santa had arrived.

We crept around the newel post and sneaked into the living room. Santa Claus had piled presents under the tree and two large, red flannel stockings hung from the fireplace mantel. We reached for the stuffed stockings and sat quietly on the floor, grasping the items inside: soap, toothpaste, toothbrush, comb, hairbrush, playing cards, candy, and colorful hair ribbons. In the toe of each stocking was a silver dollar. After we inspected the contents, we restuffed the stockings and hung them back on the mantel. Now it was time to wake Mom and Dad.

"No, it's too early," Dad complained. "Go back to bed."

"I'll make breakfast," Mom said as she hauled herself from under the bedcovers and put on a bathrobe. "That'll give you another hour."

———

With his daughters in their new nightgowns and Dad in his pajamas, we sat around the kitchen table and ate our breakfast. Then we raced to the living room, scattering ourselves around the Christmas tree. Dad handed out individual presents and sat back, smoking a cigarette, to gaze at his three girls and his loving wife. With snow falling fast and furious outside, he watched his family open presents, one at a time, oohing and aahing at every gift.

"Have you seen what's happening outside?" Dad said as he turned and glanced out the living room window. "The snow's really coming down."

# AFTER THE SNOWSTORM

We heard on the radio about the last time Connecticut had suffered such a blizzard. It was in 1888. The present storm completely paralyzed New York City, stranding cars and buses, shutting down the subway and train services. Dad had taken the Christmas holiday off and wasn't expected back to work until Monday when everything was projected to be back to normal. It wasn't. Ten-foot-high piles of snow ballooned throughout the City.

When the snowstorm passed a day later, we climbed into snowsuits, zippers pulled to the base of our throats, and ventured into the backyard. Gusting snow sliced through branches, covering the ground, coming up to our knees. Betsy and Mimi joined us, pounding snow into balls, rolling them round and round in the yard until they were about two feet in diameter. With the help of the other three, I lifted a snowball onto the large lump we used as the base. Virginia picked up the smallest snowball and placed it on the very top.

"Mom, do you have a hat?" I called into the house.

"Why do you need a hat? Oh, I see. Sure, I'll get one."

When she returned, she had one of Dad's outdated hats that had hung near the cellar steps. She also handed me a carrot and an old scarf.

Virginia dug through the snow and found a bunch of dark pebbles from our driveway. She created two eyes and a welcoming smile. I gave her the hat, carrot, and scarf. He didn't have any branches for arms but our snowman looked rather dapper in Dad's black felt hat with a navy scarf wrapped around his neck.

"Mom. Come see," I shouted.

She exited the back porch with her ever-ready camera and snapped pictures of us standing beside our creation. Four excited girls and a smiling snowman.

———————

A day later, when the snow had hardened and sun lit the frost on the trees, the Johnston siblings arrived with their sleds, knocking at our backdoor.

"Come on!" Jane said, trailing her Flexible Flyer. "We're going sledding."

The best place to sled was at the hill on Woodland Drive, on the road in front of Miss Mason's brick home. She wore her white hair in a tight bun at the nape of her neck and taught at Royle Elementary School. Her father had bought all the land in our neighborhood at the turn of the century. He built her house in the early 1920s, the first one in our section of Noroton.

At the top of the hill, we flopped on sleds and pushed off, grabbing the front wooden handles to steer. The red metal runners sliced over the icy road as we flew down the hill. Once at the bottom, we stood and grabbed our sled's rope and trudged back up the hill. Then a contest began.

"On your mark, get set, go!" Jane shouted.

We raced each other, launching our sleds to see who would reach the bottom first and who would slide the furthest. Over and over, we slid down the hill and walked back up, clouds of warm breath streaming from our mouths. Robbie and Ginny Johnston left for home, leaving five girls to continue the challenge.

Before long, the Beach Drive boys arrived at the hill. They ambushed us with snowballs and the fight was on. We grabbed handfuls of snow, mushing them into balls and compiling a stockpile on our sleds. Behind snowbanks, we bombarded each other. Jacque stood as still as a statue, saturated in snow. Despite the frost on his face, he raised his eyelids, squinted, and tossed a snowball directly at us, unleashing another assault. Yelling and throwing snowballs, we were wrapped in white globs, covered from head to toe.

"Enough!" Miss Mason shouted from her front steps. "Go home. I won't have any fighting here!"

Being a teacher with a commanding voice, we did as she asked. I grabbed my sled rope and joined Jane, Virginia, Betsy, and Mimi as we trudged back to our homes, shivering, our clothes wet with snow, our mittens saturated and cold. We followed Johnny, Gene, Dave, and Jacque who hooted and hollered about being the toughest guys in the neighborhood. Four rough and threatening boys against five strong and robust girls. Yes, they were the toughest. No doubt about it.

The snow from the Christmas storm of 1947 completely covered Darien and never fully melted until the following March.

# WATER AND ELECTRICITY

Six months later in the middle of summer, Virginia and I returned from a day at the beach. We sprayed saltwater from our bodies and chased each other around the backyard, laughing and drenching one another with water from the garden hose. Finally, Mom brought us towels and turned off the spigot. We dried ourselves and ran inside. Once out of our bathing suits and dressed in dungarees, Dad called us for dinner.

Later that night, I decided to wash my feet before climbing into bed. I scrambled onto the wicker clothes hamper, stuffed into the corner of the bathroom, and pulled myself onto the sink. Sitting on the edge with my feet in the sink, I twisted both porcelain faucet handles and felt the water washing over my legs and feet. Using a bar of Ivory soap, I scrubbed between my toes. With my feet in the water, I reached for the brass chain dangling from a sconce next to the medicine cabinet. I pulled the light chain and the room exploded. A bright flash illuminated the walls. I was thrown from the sink, landing with a thud on the tile floor.

Hearing the sound, my parents raced up the stairs to the bathroom. There I lay, a heap on the floor, moaning and crying.

"What happened?" Mom asked as she picked me from the floor and wrapped me in a towel.

"I don't know."

"What were you doing?"

"I was washing my feet. I wanted them clean before going to bed."

"Did you fall from the sink?"

"No. I turned on the light so I could see my toes better."

"That's it," Dad said. "These lights aren't grounded. I'll fix them tomorrow. In the meantime, no turning on lights with your feet in water!"

He removed the bulbs from both sconces and taped the light chains to the brass backplate. Mom escorted me to my room and helped me put on my pink nightgown. She perched on the bed while I knelt and said my prayers. With another hug, she tucked me in, opened a window, and turned on my desk light. As she left, Dad leaned into the room, and whispered his nightly mantra, "Sleep tight. Don't let the bedbugs bite."

I was alive and all was good.

# RUNNING AWAY

"Don't ever talk to me like that again," Mom scolded as she pulled me toward the kitchen sink and had me stand on a stool. She reached for a small bar of soap, resting in the metal container between the faucet handles. Mom turned on the cold water and wet the soap. Leaning me over the sink, she pushed the soap into my mouth.

"Stop," I cried as I spit out the cleansing bubbles.

"Don't ever use those words again. Now go to your room."

I raced away and ran up the stairs, crying the whole time. As soon as I reached my room, I realized Dad would probably give me a spanking when he got home. Never. I'd run away.

Inside the back of my closet was a small blue suitcase. I pulled it out, undid the two brass clasps, and stuffed it with my nightie, a pair of underpants, a Dick and Jane book, a toothbrush, and a toy animal.

With Mom ironing in the basement, I knew she'd be there for some time. She ironed everything — sheets, handkerchiefs, clothes, and even Dad's boxer shorts. I crept down the stairs, left by the backdoor, and walked up Woodland Drive. Lucky followed me as I rounded the corner at Stanley High's house and marched up Nearwater Lane. Carrying my little suitcase by its leather handle and wearing dungarees and a shirt, I continued to the traffic light and paused. After waiting for the busy, four-lane Post Road traffic to stop, I crossed and trudged up Noroton Avenue. Lucky and I hadn't gone many steps before a black and white patrol car with two officers inside pulled to the curb beside us.

"Where're you going?" one of the policemen asked after he had rolled down his window.

"I'm running away."

"Why?" he said, smiling at me, leaning his elbow out the window.

"Mom's mean. She washed my mouth out with soap."

"Why'd she do that?"

"I don't know. She's just mean."

"What's your dog's name?"

"Lucky," I said as I tugged at his collar and pulled him closer.

The policeman opened his door and stepped out. His tight, blue uniform showed a muscular build that towered over me. He scared me but his smile was reassuring. As he came closer, Lucky wagged his tail. He must not be a stranger; I guessed I was okay.

"Let's get you home. I think your mother's worried."

When the car roared to life, turned around and headed back to the Post Road, I stood on the back floor and pointed the way home. They drove to my house, parked the patrol car, and escorted Lucky and me toward the front door. My feet felt heavy, they seemed to have been dipped in cement. Along the flagstone steps we went.

It wasn't long before Mom answered the sound of the brass knocker, its gold color gleaming in the afternoon sun. She unlocked the door and looked at the two officers.

"We thought you'd want her back," one of them said.

"My gosh. I didn't even know she was gone. I was in the basement ironing," Mom said as she knelt and hugged me.

"We found her walking up Noroton Avenue," one of the officers stated. "She said you were 'mean.' But if she was mine, I'd give her a spanking."

"Thank you so much for bringing her back," Mom said, smiling politely at the two men as she ushered me inside. Once the door was closed, I was again relegated to my bedroom. This time Mom joined me, sitting on my bed, and told me about the scary things that could happen when a child runs away.

"Will you tell Dad?" I asked.

"Yes."

"Will he spank me?"

"No. I think you've learned your lesson. But he'll want to talk to you."

*Oh, no*, I thought. *Not another talking.*

After dinner Dad, Virginia, and I sat on Virginia's bed, our backs against the wall. We sat like that most nights as this was our time to read the newspaper comics while Mom cleaned the kitchen.

"I want you both to know how dangerous it is to run away from home. Or even to go away from our neighborhood," Dad said. "Our neighbors know you and could help if anything bad happened. But once you're away, there's no one who can protect you."

"What would happen?" Virginia asked.

"There are evil people everywhere. You know not to talk to strangers. You never know who's really good or bad. I want you to always stay close to home. You promise?"

"Yes," we said. Virginia looked straight into Dad's eyes while I stared at my legs, protruding across the bed. I felt uncomfortable but I knew Dad was right.

# THE BABYSITTER

The morning sun was already high in the sky the following month. Virginia and I left the house to explore and spend the remaining afternoon in the woods. We met Jane at the stump. The two girls decided to measure the circumference of the trunk's bottom. Putting our left toe behind the right heel, we walked, one at a time, around the bottom edge. Virginia and Jane came up with thirty feet, I counted thirty-five. Of course, our feet were smaller than twelve inches but they decided my measurement, as a six-year-old, was completely wrong. Yet they were the ones who counted out loud as I walked around the stump's base. Feeling hurt by their laughter and ridicule, I decided to go home.

"Hey, Barbara. Want to play?" Eddie asked as he strolled across our backyard. He was in his early teens and one of my beloved babysitters. I gladly agreed. If my sister wouldn't play with me, Eddie would. I chased after him as he walked behind several houses. Long, flimsy fingers of a willow tree in his backyard draped across my shoulders as we passed underneath. I followed him into his kitchen, through the dining room, up the front stairs and into his parents' bedroom.

"Here, Barbara. Get on the bed. We'll play a game. It'll be fun."

He reached over and picked me up. When I was settled, he flopped on the high bed and lay on his back with his head on a pillow.

"Sit on my knees and face me," he said. "I'll be a rocking horse."

I did as he asked and watched him move his body, squirming to just the right position. I wondered what we were going to play.

"Come closer. Sit here," he said as he patted his thighs. When I moved as he wanted, he began to lift his thighs. Slowly, in a steady beat, he bounced me up and down. I giggled and raised my hands high over my head. Laughing with complete abandon, I yelled "Faster! Faster!"

Eddie, pleased by my wild reaction, began to raise and lower his thighs in an undulating rhythm. His tongue flicked at the corner of his mouth and he licked his lips. I saw his fingers unzip his dungarees; white underpants peeked back at me. As his hips pulsated, he roughly cupped the back of my head, and forcibly pulled my head down, pushing my face to his groin.

*What was he doing?* I wanted to be his friend, but this felt creepy, even wrong. Terror found its way into my mind and I twisted away from his grasp, fleeing the room. In a flash I was down the stairs and out the backdoor, running behind neighboring houses toward my backdoor.

No one was home when I entered the house. Breathing hard I ran through the kitchen and dining room, up the stairs, and fled to the security of our bathroom. As soon as I could, I slammed the door and turned the metal deadbolt, locking the door. Recoiling, I wedged myself in the far corner, between the tub and radiator. With a towel wrapped around me, I hugged my knees to my chest, forming a little cocoon of comfort as I shivered. I laced my fingers together to keep my hands from shaking and waited.

I heard him in the upstairs hallway. The floor before the bathroom door complained beneath his weight as I listened. *He's here.* Eddie wrapped his fingers around the glass knob, rattled it and twisted; but he couldn't open the door. The hairs on the back of my neck bristled, fear pulsed and crept up my spine. My tongue felt dry. I held my breath.

"Open up, Barbara. I want to talk."

"No. Go away."

"I didn't mean anything. I just wanted to play," Eddie said through the closed door.

"Go away!"

"I'm really sorry," Eddie pleaded. "Promise you won't tell?"

"I won't. Go away," I said. "I won't come out 'til you leave."

I heard him on the landing, turning and going down the stairs. Once the backdoor shut, I began to calm. But I still didn't come out of the bathroom. I sat in stunned silence on the tile floor. My mind scrambled to figure out what had happened. I listened and listened. And probably waited another half hour before I unlocked the door. I slipped out of the bathroom, stood in the hallway, and hesitated. I crept down the stairs and pressed my palms against the glass of the French doors leading to the back porch.

*Is he gone?* Hearing rustling in the kitchen, I knew Mom was home. Safe at last.

Although I never did tell anyone about the incident, Eddie no longer babysat for our family. After his father died, they moved to another town, further up the Connecticut coast. My memory of the incident was locked away, repressed, not to emerge until I mentioned it to my sister years later, when I was forty.

# KNIVES, GUNS, AND BOMBS

We carried metal lunch boxes stuffed with snacks, sandwiches, and a milk-filled thermos to elementary school. The outside boxes had colorful drawings of popular cowboys: Hopalong Cassidy, the Lone Ranger, Roy Rogers. We also brought knives to our classrooms. Pocket knives with two- or three-inch blades. Mine was black with a hammered handle and a single blade.

During recess we often dangled from the monkey bars or chased each other, playing tag in the playground. But our favorite game was Mumblety-peg, locally known as "Split."

Karen and I stood facing each other, about two feet apart, our heels and toes in alignment. With a flick of her wrist, Karen, one of my best friends at Hindley, shot her knife toward the ground. If the blade penetrated the dirt, I had to spread my legs, moving my foot to her knife, keeping my other foot in its original position. Next, I took my knife and attempted the same move in the opposite direction. If it stuck, Karen had to step to my knife. We took turns with our knives and continued the game until one of us could no longer stretch to the opposing knife. At no time did the teachers or parents think this was a dangerous game.

When the outdoor bell sounded, we ran back to class. The walls over the blackboards were covered with white paper mats. Alphabet letters, capital and lowercase images, printed in black ink. Knowing these letters and looking at books filled with pictures, we started to read. *A is for Apple, B is for Bus, C is for Cat*. And we learned how to spell our state, Connecticut. "Connect, I, Cut."

One of our teachers asked us to line up for a spelling contest. She touched the top of our heads as she walked the row of students, and called, "Eeny, meeny, miney, moe. Catch a nigger by the toe. If he hollers, let him go, eeny, meeny, miney, moe." At her touch during the last word that child was selected to be the captain of the spelling bee. She uttered the same rhyme for the second captain. To us it was just a jingle; the words meant nothing.

———

In 1950 the Union of Soviet Socialist Republics (USSR) announced possession of an atomic bomb. When an alarm bell sounded, we filed into the hallway, the classroom door shut behind us. We stood with our backs to the wall and slowly sank to the floor, squatting with our knees pulled to our chests. We huddled and whispered until another bell sounded and we returned to our class.

We had participated in an air raid drill, our introduction to the Cold War and its repercussions. The Soviet Union versus the United States. During Hindley's bomb protection practice, some children stayed in their classrooms and participated in "duck and cover," hiding under their desks, providing a slight degree of protection outside the radius of a nuclear explosion. Teachers and parents talked about buying gas masks and building underground bunkers. It wasn't scary because we didn't understand the magnitude of the situation. It was just something Hindley Elementary required us to do.

═══════

On the way home, we hid behind bushes and tugged guns from leather holsters. Metal cap guns, loaded with red tape cap rolls, gave realistic sounds. Crouching and yelling, we shot at each other. Good guys and bad, cowboys at their best. We shot our pistols and ran bent over, running for cover behind bush after bush. Exciting blasts and puffs of smoke as we bombarded one another. In elementary school guns and knives were our daily delights. No one questioned our passions.

# HOLLY POND IN WINTER

"Can Susan come out and play?" I asked Mrs. Fedlar that next January while standing on their front porch. Snow slowly drifted from bare branches near their house, sparkling in the breeze with just a hint from the sun.

"She's putting on her coat now. Why don't you come in and wait?"

I stepped inside and stood in the foyer, glancing into their two-story living room. Susan came down the hall from the maid's room, now used as her father's office. She wore rubber boots, snow pants, a heavy jacket, and a wool hat. I was similarly dressed.

The day was sunny and cold, a perfect day to explore. Light blowing snow looked magical against the spruce trees. We were in heaven. Susan waved to her mother as we walked south on Outlook Drive. No one careened on sleds or toboggans over the sloping field across from the Johnston's brick house. The street was deserted. We continued down the hill toward Beach Drive. The road had not yet been plowed and our boots crunched on icy snow. We turned left, past Alison's house on the corner, and then tramped to the end of the private lane. I had a mission in mind.

We saw Holly Pond ahead of us, frozen and inviting. Susan and I scrambled over a three-foot-high stone wall and trudged through deep snow. A chilly breeze whipped in from Long Island Sound. Snowflakes danced in the wind, surrounding us.

"Come on, Susan," I said. "Let's see what it's like to skate on the pond."

"I don't think my parents want me on the ice," she said.

"It's all right. It's frozen solid, Come on. Let's go."

Wanting to please, she followed me to the pond's edge. The two of us stepped on the ice. Not hearing any cracking of weak ice, we proceeded around the large, saltwater inlet. Every twenty feet or so a high pile of snow protruded from the ice. They looked like white, plump pillows.

"That looks soft. Almost like a cloud," I said pointing to a white blob.

"Do you think it's soft?" Susan asked.

"I don't know. Why don't you jump in and see?"

"Okay. But don't tell my parents," Susan said.

She bent her knees, threw her hands in the air, and took a giant leap. Giant, that is, for a seven-year-old. High above the soft mound, she soared, smashing into the middle of the snow pile. I watched, impressed with her amazing jump.

Susan crashed through the mound, exploding snow blasting upward and outward. Instantly, she plunged into the freezing water. Her elbows, caught on the surrounding ice, kept her from falling deeper.

"Help me," she screamed, her frightened eyes bulging in fear. Strands of dark brown hair stuck to her cheek as she began to cry. Only her upper jacket and wool hat showed above the ice. The rest of her clothes were below the ice. They began to soak up water, pulling her into the pond's icy grasp.

I seized the arm of her wool jacket and tugged. And tugged. Slowly dragging her from the water. Exhausted, Susan lay on the ice and sobbed, her head resting on her folded arms.

"I'm freezing," she stammered. "Mom's going to be really mad."

Hauling her away from the ice, I put my arm around her waist and half dragged her back to the stone wall. She shivered in her wet clothes as we clambered over rough crags and slogged through heavy snow, struggling back to the road. Slowly we stumbled the way we had come, up the hill to her home as stray snowflakes continued to float by us.

A loud groan escaped the hinges as Susan opened her heavy, front door. Deep inside the house, we heard footfalls and then a voice.

"Why are you home so early?" Mrs. Fedlar asked.

"I didn't mean it, Mom," Susan called into the house. "Honest!"

"What happened?" she asked as she knelt and began to unwrap wet clothes from her daughter.

"We were walking on Holly Pond and I fell in," Susan whimpered, as fresh tears flowed down her cheeks.

"What happened, Barbara?" Mrs. Fedlar demanded, turning to face me. I stood next to Susan and looked at my boots.

"I don't know," I said. "Susan jumped into a pile of snow and she fell through the ice."

"Why were you on the ice anyway, Susan? You know you're not allowed to do that. Let's get you into a bath and warm you up. And Barbara, I don't think Susan will be playing with you for quite some time!"

She turned me around and gently, but firmly, pushed me from the foyer, closing the front door behind me. I could hear Susan crying and saying it wasn't her fault. Now I knew I was in trouble. When I reached home, Mrs. Fedlar had already telephoned my mother.

Mom met me in the kitchen, a serious expression on her face. "Why were you on the ice? You know how dangerous it is."

"But, Mom. It was frozen solid."

"Then how did Susan fall in?"

"She jumped into a snow pile. We didn't know there wasn't any ice under the snow."

"And why did she jump into the snow?"

"I guess I asked her to," I mumbled.

"Yes, I guess that's probably right. Let's get you out of your boots and jacket. Then you can go to your room and think about what happened with Susan today."

"It wasn't that bad," I said. "She'll warm up."

"No, Barbara. That's not right. There's a reason we ask you not to go on the ice," Mom said as she removed my outer clothes. "Holly Pond is saltwater and it never completely freezes. Susan is lucky. She could have fallen completely through. You wouldn't have been able to pull her out. And the ice edge could have broken. Then you both would have been in the water and both of you could have drowned!" She took a deep breath, "I'm ashamed of you."

I crawled up the stairs to my bedroom, tears welling in my eyes. *Why did I have to make mistakes? Why couldn't I know right from wrong? When will I ever learn?*

# BROOM BALL

Spring blossomed into summer and our family introduced the neighborhood to Broom Ball. Using the flat of a broom to hit a pitched tennis ball, the batter held the handle and swung. Once the ball was hit, the batter ran the bases. No need for mitts or great athletic ability. Almost anyone could play.

The Austin, Hazelton, and Johnston kids gathered in our backyard one hot afternoon. The lawn had been cut and the bases laid out. The children hit the ball, ran the bases, and cheered their team. The sun was high overhead but the breeze from the Sound kept the day cool, a perfect day for Broom Ball. Leaves rustled in the canopies and birds chirped on branches as we encouraged our runners to keep moving, to keep running the bases.

"Come home," we yelled. "Come home."

But the catcher caught the ball and the runner was out. Mom had gone inside to make Kool-Aid when I was chosen to be the pitcher in the next inning. I stood close to home plate as I was only eight and didn't have much of a throwing arm. Winding up for an underhand pitch, batter after batter hit the ball but never made it to first base. Jane was in the outfield and Virginia stood at first base. What a team we had. Two up and two out.

Dad came to home plate, took the broom by the handle, and swung it a couple of times, warming up. He told the outfield to be ready. He was going to hit a "high fly." Everyone stood at attention and I felt nervous. With a lob of my hand, I pitched the ball to my father. He swung hard and smashed the ball with the firm section of the broom, not the bristles.

The ball zoomed through the air. Rocketing straight for me. It smashed into my forehead. My knees buckled and I fell to the ground, instantly knocked out. I learned later that everyone had remained frozen, no one had moved. They were shocked. A split second later, Dad rushed to me, carrying my limp body to the hammock. Betsy ran inside to alert Mom. She came out with a wet washcloth and the Kool-Aid she had just made.

I awoke in our hammock, pale as an egg. My vision blurred and my head pounded, a cluster of kids stared at me. Mom placed the cold washcloth on my forehead, over the purple knot beginning to form.

"How do you feel?" Mom asked.

"What happened?" I asked.

Dad reiterated the event while Mom lifted my head and pressed a glass of Kool-Aid to my lips. I took a few sips and said, "I have a headache."

"Just lie here for a few minutes. I'll get you an aspirin."

Dad stood over me, worried. He lifted me from the hammock, carrying me close to his chest, my head resting on his shoulder. To the back porch, inside, and up the stairs to my bedroom. It was a fun day in spite of the accident. An almost perfect day for Broom Ball.

# COMIC BOOK INCIDENT

"You do that again and I'll tell your father," he said. The large man behind the counter stared down at me and took a dime from my sweaty palm. He removed a *Donald Duck* comic book from inside an *Archie* comic book. In my dungarees and plaid shirt, I peeked over the candy counter and looked up at him, flushed with embarrassment. I had tried to steal a comic book by putting one inside the other, paying only for the outer one.

"I won't do that again. Honest," I whispered. "I'm really sorry,"

Lowering my head and turning away, I walked from the counter, past shelves stacked with toys and games, books and cigarettes, newspapers and magazines. With the comic book in a paper sack under my arm and staring at the oak floor, I felt his eyes boring into the back of my head. I trudged toward the exit. The bell tied above the shop door rang as I departed the store.

This was my first time walking by myself to buy something at the Puritan Stationery Store. I had collected a few discarded soda and beer bottles from alongside the roads and had returned them next door at the grocery store. They gave me a penny or two for each one I brought in, depending on its size.

As an eight-year-old and with money in my pocket, I felt like a big kid. Ashamed about the comic book incident, I left the Puritan, my head down, tears choking my eyes. Standing on the corner of the Post Road and Noroton Avenue, waiting for the light to change, I knew everyone was staring and me, pointing at the little girl who tried to steal. Thief! Robber!

He never said a word to my father. And I never stole again. The owner always greeted me with a friendly smile whenever I went back into his store. He taught me to be honest, to be truthful. It was a good lesson.

# BLACKBERRIES

Mom gathered us in the car and drove to Brush Island Road near the end of Nearwater Lane. Small silver buckets rested at our feet. We were excited. It was a hot, August afternoon when we arrived at the wild blackberry patch. My sisters, Mom, and I slipped out of the car and circled a large area, covered with ripe blackberries exploding from prickly branches, protected by spiky thorns.

Nearby honeysuckle, its yellow blooms alive with the sound of bees, stopped us in our tracks. We watched them mine the flowers, gathering honey and flying back to their nests. We gave them a wide berth and headed to the blackberries.

Walking around and leaning into the thick bushes, we slowly filled our pails with berries, some as big as our thumbs. Blackbirds squawked above us, upset that we had invaded their territory. Briars snagged our clothes and hands. Virginia, Gail, and I plunked many of the juicy berries into our mouths, and before long our faces and hands were smeared with reddish-black liquid. We looked like clowns when we walked back to the car.

"Let's wipe your hands before you get inside," Mom said.

We stood with our hands extended while she scrubbed them clean. Then she took a towel and wiped our faces. Large cumulus clouds began to jostle against each other and rolled across a darkening sky. Damp smells surrounded us as we piled into the car. With the buckets secured by our feet, we left the blackberry bushes and headed for home. A summer rain drummed against the car's roof and drops collected in puddles. A steady rain fell in a thin curtain, obscuring our view, as we continued over the soggy dirt road. Mom shifted to low gear, avoiding numerous potholes and several deep ruts.

In the back seat, Virginia and I played "rock, paper, scissors," tossing out our hands as a fist, a flat hand, or extended fingers, acting as scissors. Virginia won as she produced a "paper" which covered my closed fist. This meant she had first dibs in the bathtub that night. Saturday night was bath night. Mom and Dad wanted us sparkling clean for church on Sunday. As we turned from Nearwater Lane to Woodland Drive, the rain stopped. It was only a quick shower. Heat visibly rose from the road and a stunning mirage appeared.

"Look at that," Mom said.

We knelt on our seats and looked out the front window. In the middle of the road, a giant pond had been created, black and imposing.

"What's that?" Virginia asked.

"It's a mirage," Mom said. "We'll look it up after dinner. Mom was the local salesperson for the World Book Encyclopedia Company, and, consequently, encouraged us to look up any new word or subject.

# THE LAST SUPPER

It was ninety degrees in the waning days of summer that year. We placed our leather suitcases behind the car and stood in shorts and tee shirts, looking at Dad. He selected several cases and neatly packed the trunk, already loaded with sleeping bags and boxes of food.

Mom saw us standing behind the car and yelled from the porch, "Go to the bathroom."

"I don't have to go," I said.

"Go anyway."

We three sisters traipsed back into the house and took turns in the downstairs bathroom. When we reappeared, Dad said, "Okay, girls. Get in."

"Here's our lunch," Mom said as she entered the car, carrying a basket covered with an embroidered tea towel.

Virginia and I sat in the backseat with Lucky; Gail was placed up front between Dad and Mom. Dad reversed the car and backed into our turn-around space before heading out the driveway to the Boston Post Road. Steering toward Norwalk, he selected Route 7 North, past Danbury to northwestern Connecticut.

Mom had already booked two nights for us at a small cabin near the north end of Candlewood Lake. It was Labor Day weekend and she wanted to be sure we had a place to stay. As we drove along the scenic highway, we began to sing. "Don't Sit Under the Apple Tree with Anyone Else but Me." Mom knew the words but sang off-key; Dad had a beautiful voice and we eagerly joined our parents for the chorus. Typically, we learned songs from the thirties, the era of Mom and Dad.

Wind passed through the wing vents and all four of our open windows, helping to cool the car. Dad periodically flicked cigarette ashes out the front triangular window as we drove north and wandered along a small road into the Berkshire Mountains. It was a sun-filled day, a wonderful day for a picnic.

"Here's the spot," Mom said.

We looked out the window and stared at a high wooden structure.

"What is it?" Virginia asked.

"It's a fire tower. Men climb to the top to see if there's a fire in the forest."

"What? You want to have a picnic on the look-out?" Dad asked.

"Sure. It'll be fun."

"I don't think we're allowed to do this."

"Oh, they won't mind. We'll have our lunch and be back to our car in no time."

Mom often pushed traditional rules to the limit, making life unpredictable for her family. Surprisingly, Dad went along with her impulses, not always but often enough for us to have many adventurous outings. She made her mark on our family by being a fountain of enthusiasm, enriching most experiences with her eagerness and passion. She urged us to explore, maybe to be a little different, and to take chances.

We piled out of the car and let Lucky do his business. Then I placed him back in the Chevy. After Dad parked the car in the shade of a maple tree and all the windows were rolled halfway down, Lucky peered out, his jaw resting on a windowpane. We trudged to the bottom of the ladder and stopped. The above platform seemed so far away. *Could we actually make it to the top?* My doubts were rinsed away by Mom's excitement.

"Not to worry. It'll be fun!" Mom said as Virginia started up the ladder, embracing a leap of faith.

"Okay, Turkey Legs, you're next," Dad said. I knew that meant me. He often teased me as I had long, thin legs. But I liked the nickname. I grasped each rung, pulling myself up until I reached the platform, almost fifty feet above the ground.

Gail climbed next with Mom's arms wrapped around her. She was only five but she was fearless. They scaled the ladder, looking like two crabs, one on top of the other. Dad had switched the lunch from the basket to a beach towel and tightly wrapped it around his body. He used both hands to ascend the steep ladder.

At last, we were on the wooden platform of the fire look-out tower, high in the air. We stood and looked at the view. The sky shined a crystalline blue. Mountain ridges undulated in the distance; leaves had begun to turn several shades of red, orange, and yellow. Colors haphazardly mingled with green spruce trees. Nature's kaleidoscope.

"Isn't this beautiful?" Mom said smiling. "Anyone can have a picnic on the ground but how many can have one with this view?"

Dad grunted but didn't say anything. We perched ourselves in a circle as close to the center of the platform as possible. Because we sat below the railing, nothing obstructed our view. And nothing stopped us from falling over the edge. Mom passed out peanut butter and jelly sandwiches enclosed in white napkins along with several carrot slices. Dad poured milk from his thermos into waiting paper cups as we sat nervously unwrapping the sandwiches.

"Not peanut butter and jelly," I moaned. "We have that every day."

"Beggars can't be choosers," Mom said. "Now eat up."

Slowly and deliberately, we completed our meal, chewing the carrot sticks and drinking milk. Huddled together high in the sky, Mom was exuberant.

"I can't get over how beautiful it is. We're so lucky to be here."

"Fine. But I certainly don't want to do this again," Dad said after we finished our lunch. "Hopefully we can get down as easily as we got up."

"I'll go first," Mom said. "Gail, you come next. Turn around and slowly back toward me. We'll go down as a twosome."

Dad went next and waited for me. I crawled backward until I reached the ladder. Backing over the edge was terrifying. Treacherous thoughts wormed their way into my head. *Would I fall? Could I hang on? Would I die?* I looked at Virginia standing alone on the platform and tried to focus. Dad gripped my right foot and put it on the top step. He guided my left foot to the same step and then wrapped his arms around me. We took three steps and stopped. Virginia did as I did. She crept backward until she came to the edge. Holding onto the railing, her feet touched the ladder. The three of us descended like one group. As Virginia was ten, she seemed very confident. I, however, was scared to death.

"Wasn't that fun!" Mom said. Now that we were on the ground, our enthusiasm reappeared. Lucky barked, sending a greeting and asking to be let out. I raced to the Chevy and let Lucky run through a pasture. He ran in circles around our family, so glad to see us safely on the ground.

Driving from the tower back to the rented cabin, Dad decided on a title for our picnic.

"Let's call it, 'The Last Supper.'"

We laughed at the name much to the chagrin of Mom. Although it had no significance to Leonardo's painting, the thought of falling over the platform's edge created an indelible impression on me as the last supper for the Phelps family.

# THE ATTIC AND BASEMENT

When days became gloomy as autumn approached, Virginia and I played in either the attic or basement, large areas to occupy ourselves while waiting for the weather to change.

Clouds bustled against each other and drops of rain began to fall. Dottie and Sally, Virginia's best friends from elementary school, joined us in the attic: building a farm with plastic cowboy and Indian figures, farm animals, and barns. We used popsicle sticks to make fences around an elaborate ranch. Bow-legged figures easily fit on top of the horses. Miniature trees and shrubs abutted the barns. Even tiny plastic chickens found their way beside the cows and pigs. We sprawled on an old, red-patterned carpet, letting our imagination run rampant.

On the other side of the attic staircase, two black steamer trunks with steel bands and hinges rested under the back slant of the roof. They were low enough to slide under a ship's bunk and came from Mom's year-long stay at a finishing school in Italy. Stuffed with black and white pictures and postcards illustrating her travels around Europe, the four of us inspected her keepsakes, imagining what it was like to ski in the Alps or attend lavish parties in extravagant gowns.

In the far corner stood a stack of National Geographic Magazines. When it came time to write a school assignment,

I used scissors to cut images from the magazines and taped them to pages, illustrating my writing project. Mountains, animals, jungles, deserts, oceans. But what really intrigued me were the photographs of bare-breasted women from Africa. I stared at them. *So that's what a woman looks like.* I wondered if I might have a body like theirs when I became older.

---

Months later, the dark earth steamed from a spring thunderstorm. I telephoned Jeannie Hazelton, a nearby neighbor, and asked her to come over to play.

"Sure. Do you want me to bring my skates? How about Betsy McCall?"

"Yes. It's an icky day. Bring them both."

As rain raced through our downspouts, Jeannie joined me in the attic with her Betsy McCall paper dolls. We had both removed images of "Betsy" from the last page of *McCall's* monthly magazine. We also cut several paper outfits and their appropriate accessories from the magazine. We bent the white tabs on top of each outfit to fit over Betsy's shoulders, preparing her for the beach, or maybe a party, or a picnic, or shopping. We played for an hour or so and then joined Virginia and Gail in the basement.

Jeannie had earlier carried her metal roller skates in a canvas carryall to the back porch. Gathering her bag, she walked with me through the kitchen and down the wooden stairs curving to the basement. We sat on the bottom steps and adjusted skates to our shoes, wrapping and buckling a leather strap around each ankle. Using a metal key, we tightened the front skate grips to our shoes and then hung the key's string around our necks. Now we were ready.

Following Virginia and Gail, we skated round and round, using our hands on the house's support posts to swing to the other side of the basement. Then bending down into a compact circle and scooting fast under the ping pong table. The four of us skated and laughed until we were out of breath. Our attic and basement areas were perfect places to play, especially during inclement weather.

# PEN PALS

Miss Peebles, a pretty woman in her twenties, with dark brown hair and freckles, taught my third-grade class. Besides reading and writing, she introduced us to science: the solar system and geographic features of several countries. She also taught my favorite subject: mathematics. Division and multiplication. Nine times nine, twelve times three, fifteen times four. And she made math fun. She showed us how to fold paper into triangles, making cootie catchers to tease other students.

On bad weather days when we couldn't go outside and didn't want to read in our classroom, we lined the hall floors and played jacks. Throwing a little red ball high in the air and scooping up the six-pointed, metal jacks.

At the end of each day, Miss Peebles kissed every one of her students on the cheek. Even the rowdies who had originally been spanked by Mrs. Milano. I think everyone loved her.

In October, Miss Peebles presented us with a list of Japanese pen pals. I chose Sumiko Hatta and scribbled a letter to her on thin, blue Airmail paper, one that folded into an envelope.

*Dear Pen Pal Friend,*

*I am in Third Grade. I am eight years old. I have two sisters and a dog named Lucky.*

*What do you like to do? I like to ride horses and play outside. Where do you live? I live in Connecticut, near the Atlantic Ocean.*

*Goodbye for now. Please write soon.*

*Your friend, Barbara Phelps*

---

*Dear Barbara,*

*I am in ninth grade. I am fourteen years old and I have a brother. I like to read and sing. I play several instruments. I study hard in school and want to travel. Maybe I can visit you?*

*I live in a city, near a river and a sea. I look forward to your next letter.*

*Your Pen Pal, Sumiko Hatta*

I wrote every month to Sumiko, a girl who lived in Kanazawa, a beautiful section of Japan bordering the Sea of Japan. She wrote back just as often. From Miss Peebles I learned that in the early 1900s, the Tokyo mayor sent Washington, D.C., a gift of Yoshino cherry trees. The United States reciprocated with flowering dogwood trees.

"These are the cherry blossoms we see each spring at the capital," she informed us.

---

As icicles slipped from tree limbs, winter days shortened and spring pansies began to show their heads.

Mom surprised us with a long-haired, white kitten. In my subsequent letter to Sumiko, I asked her if she would like to name it. She did and immediately wrote back. "Shiro" became the kitten's name. The word in Japanese meant "white snow."

My interest in everything oriental began with my pen pal. One day Mom and Dad took Virginia and me to New York City's Chinatown. They purchased a pair of Chinese dolls for both of us. Each figure stood about five inches tall, dressed in typical Chinese outfits, and fit into a tiny wicker crate. The man sported a black braid dropping down his back; the woman had beads and flowers wrapped in her headband. Both wore pants with colorful, vest-type jackets falling to their knees.

While in Chinatown, they also bought me a magic box made of different types of inlaid wood, no nails and no hinges. The three-by-five-inch case had no opening I could detect, just a painting of a sailing "junk" boat and a snow-capped Mt. Fuji. Constructed only of sliding panels. I pushed one end down, moved the top a fraction, pushed the other end down, and slid the top panel off. With an empty space, I found a special spot to hide some treasures. Surprisingly, although these items were sold in Chinatown and depicted Chinese people, they were made in Japan. As Dad told us, "America has no contacts with China. Everything Chinese actually comes from Japan."

# FORSYTHIAS

When warblers returned from their winter homes in the South, forsythia's bright yellow bells heralded the awakening of spring. Their branches, we soon learned, had a wicked bite. Dad raked his fingers over a three-foot stem, deleting its pretty blossoms and letting them tumble to the ground. When any of us acted up, he'd reach for the branch and swished it across our legs, leaving a red scratch in its wake.

He kept the branch on the top of the refrigerator. If we were in the kitchen and began to be disruptive, all he had to do was look at the refrigerator's crown and we'd immediately clam up. No way did we want the Forsythia's mark on our legs.

One evening when all of us were tired from working and playing outside, Virginia ignored the warning when she boisterously entered the kitchen. She continued with her tirade until Dad had had enough.

"Quiet!" he yelled. Virginia disregarded his command. Dad grabbed the forsythia branch and chased Virginia into the dining room. All of us followed, wanting to see the outcome.

Around the table Virginia raced, again and again, with Dad right behind her. Just as Dad came close, she ran behind Mom, hiding behind her skirt. Dad's aim went awry and slashed right across Mom's ankles. Mom screamed with pain and jumped from one foot to the other. Dad dropped the switch and immediately apologized.

"I'm so sorry," he said, his head slightly bowed. Mom replaced the forsythia switch on top of the refrigerator and never said another word.

# ON THE ROOF

While lying in bed reading, I heard a knock on my window. Virginia waved to me, a gigantic smile on her face. She yelled into my room.

"Get up. Let's play."

I raised the window all the way and climbed out. The two of us sat on the tiled roof, wondering what to do next.

"Let's jump to the plum tree," Virginia said. "Then we can go to the Stump without bothering Mom."

And so, we did. We jumped from the roof of the sunroom and grabbed onto sturdy branches, descending the tree like monkeys, gripping limb after limb until we were on the ground. We exited the house by way of the plum tree so many times it became a normal route. Because Mom didn't keep close tabs on us, I don't know if she ever knew this was the way we reached the outside. As long as we were home for meals, parents didn't seem to worry about their children's outdoor activities.

When summer fell to autumn and leaves began to turn, I put on my Halloween costume to see if the black cape fit. I added a black wax mustache and looked in the bathroom mirror. Once everything was to my nine-year-old satisfaction, I walked through Mom and Dad's bedroom to Gail's room and climbed out her window.

Standing on the top of the garage roof, I grabbed the gutter over my head and threw my leg up to the clay tiles, pulling myself to the roof.

With Virginia and Gail, along with other neighbor kids, I had been on the garage roof numerous times, jumping off the back, over the forsythia bushes, and rolling on the lawn, eight feet below. But this was different; I wanted to get to the very top of the house. With bare feet and clinging toes, I crawled over the rounded tiles to the roof ridge, about thirty feet above the ground. Slowly standing, I held my arms out and felt my cape flowing backward. Perfect. With my feet straddling the ridge, I looked over treetops and saw Holly Pond and the edge of Stamford. Taking one tiny step at a time, I walked toward the end of the roof.

While outside gardening, our neighbor, Auntie Dot saw me standing high on our house roof and rushed inside to telephone Mom.

"Florence, I don't mean to alarm you but Barbara is on the roof. At the very top!"

Mom shrieked into the phone and raced up the stairs, around the top landing, through her room, and into Gail's room. Seeing the window open, she climbed out. Mom stood and braced herself, grabbing hold of the gutter, she called to me.

"Barbara, come down right now! No, don't turn around. Just bend down and crawl backward. I'll help you."

I did as she said. I bent and got on my hands and knees, my little black cape trailing behind. The tile roof scraped my legs but my bare feet held me from slipping on the crusty-coated tile. I crawled backward, inching my way on the rough ridge. With Mom's encouragement, I turned, still on my hands and knees, and gradually slid backward over the roof to her waiting arms. My mustache firmly attached below my nose.

"What were you doing?" she asked once we were inside Gail's room.

"I wanted to see how my costume worked. Whether the cape would float in the wind."

"Couldn't you do that on the ground? Don't ever do that again," she said. "You're going to be the death of me yet. And you frightened Auntie Dot. I know she's watching. I'll call her and let her know you're safe."

# CRACK THE WHIP

Icy winds whirled in from the Sound three months later, bearing a snowstorm heading toward the Northeast. We listened to the radio, waiting to hear the announcement — whether we'd have a snow day or not. Yes! No school! The plow graders were overloaded, the buses couldn't run, and the New York/New Haven train had stalled in Bridgeport.

After the worst of the storm had passed, Mom and Dad gathered the three of us and six neighborhood children for sledding over our blanketed roads. The Austin twins and four of the Johnston siblings joined us for the icy adventure. Dad took a long rope and fastened it to the wooden sleds and then to our car's bumper, about fifteen feet away. I climbed on the first sled and lay down. Nine kids all in a line behind my parents' car.

Mom climbed into the backseat and looked out the rear window, checking that we were ready to move. On the sleds, we laughed while snow drifted, falling from nearby fir trees. She told Dad it was time to go. He slowly drove up Woodland Drive and turned right on Nearwater Lane. After an uneventful sled ride, we arrived in the Noroton Bay neighborhood. No cars were on the road and Dad decided to drive faster, the Chevy bucking over the frozen, rutted road. He made a quick turn and the sleds flew in a half-circle, slamming into the side of a fluffy snowbank. Sleds and kids scattered everywhere. Laughing, we climbed back on our sleds and yelled for more.

"Do it again," we screamed, our breaths spiraling out in front of us.

And so, he did. With the Chevy sliding in snow, we zipped in circles around the informal Weed Beach area, playing "crack the whip." If you were the last one on the "whip," there was no way you could stay attached to the sled in front. The speed of eight sleds flying in a circle was too much.

"Go faster," we yelled.

Silver strands of sleet slipped from the sky, turning into large flakes of snow. It was beginning to snow again.

"Okay," Mom said. "Let's head home."

"Not yet," we begged.

But home we went, slowly heading up Nearwater Lane. Mom invited everyone in for hot chocolate with tiny marshmallows. We trooped inside, rosy-cheeked and exuberant. After dropping our outer clothes on the back porch, we sauntered into the kitchen, standing in a circle, sipping from ceramic cups. Lucky sat between us, looking up, waiting as usual, for something to fall to the floor.

# HORSESHOE CRABS

Mom rubbed Coppertone on us when we arrived at Noroton Bay Beach Club the next summer. Seaweed lay in dark clumps along the shore and I could smell and even taste the salt air. Our toes squeaked on the hot beach as Virginia, Gail, and I raced from our towels to the cooling waters of Long Island Sound. The wet sand felt crisp beneath my toes. I stepped into the water, wading knee-deep, and watched a black shadow moving along the sand, under the incoming waves. It was a horseshoe crab. To me they were scary. With so many legs, they reminded me of gigantic spiders.

"They're considered living fossils," Mom said. "They were around when we had dinosaurs."

"Wow. You'd have thought dinosaurs would have stepped on them."

"Oh, they probably did. But they're resilient. If the shell cracks, it will heal itself. But not if it's completely crushed."

"Come see this," Mom said as she picked up the crab by its tail and turned it over on the sand.

"That looks so creepy. I hate all those legs."

"They're actually very safe. They won't hurt us at all."

"Look at this," she said. We watched the brown crab struggle on its back, its legs moving a mile a minute. Then it stuck its tail into the sand and flipped itself over. Once the crab was right-side-up, it crawled back to the water. We stood staring at it, our hands on our hips, squinting in the sun.

"What else can it do?"

"I don't know, but another amazing thing is about their blood. It's blue."

"Why wouldn't their blood be red?"

"I'm not sure. We'll look them up when we get home," Mom said.

# ROBERTSON HOUSE

A few years after we moved to Outlook Drive, the Robertson family left for Mansfield Avenue. On one of our visits to their new home, Uncle Dick asked Mom and Dad to join Aunt Marty and him in the spacious front yard, planting hundreds, possibly thousands, of daffodil bulbs.

On the drive to the Robertson's home, I inserted a stick of gum in my mouth, chewing madly as we drove through tree-lined streets. I rolled down the back window and threw out the aluminum wrapper. Dad slammed on the brakes and pulled to the side of the road.

"We do *not* litter," Mom said, turning to stare at me.

With that, I was ordered out of the car and had to walk back to pick up the trash, balling it into my fist.

*What's the big deal,* I thought. But it was another lesson. One that I learned as I continued to mature. I never threw anything to the roadside again, unless it could be eaten by animals, such as apple cores or bread crusts.

When we arrived at the Robertson house, we assumed our roles. The parents and Gail planted daffodil bulbs. Virginia and Wade explored the expansive backyard and pond. I joined Polly in the house.

"I want to show you the birdcage," Polly said.

This was no ordinary birdcage but a glass room. Maybe six feet wide and three feet deep, from floor to ceiling, between a hallway and the den. Inside were bare tree branches and about a dozen birds.

"Wow. Look at all the birds. How neat is this!"

"Come look what else we have. Our own greenhouse!"

We walked down the hallway into a greenhouse filled with flowers. I had never seen orchids before and was amazed by their colors; mostly pinks, purples, and whites but a few reds and yellows. They were also in unusual shapes, some looking like angels or birds. Uncle Dick had collected them from all over the world.

Polly pushed her blond hair to the side and turned me around. She wanted to show me something in the dining room. We crawled between a couple of chairs, to the space near the head of the table. Kneeling beneath the mahogany structure, she pointed to a bump in the carpet. A large knob protruding upward.

"Take your hand and push on it," she instructed.

Using the palm of my hand, I pressed on the bulge. I sat back on my haunches and looked at Polly. Nothing happened.

"What're you two doing?" Hannah, the maid, asked as she passed through a white swinging door. Dressed in a dark uniform with a beige apron, the colored woman had flour covering her outstretched hands.

"I wanted to show Barbara how the bell works," Polly said from under the table.

"I'll show you how a switch works," Hannah said. "Now git."

Crawling out, I saw she had a sweet smile on her face but I wasn't taking any chances. We backed our way out and rushed upstairs to Polly's bedroom.

"Isn't that neat? Dad sits at the table and steps on the knob. A bell rings in the kitchen. Hannah then knows she's needed in the dining room."

Polly opened a drawer in the linen closet to show me samples of past Christmas cards, ones Uncle Dick had had crafted in Italy and had sent to our family and other close friends over the previous six years. Each large card had been drawn individually. Gold paint around the edges. The Virgin Mary and Jesus depicted in the interior. Colorful images that my mom had saved in a special box back home.

# CAPE COD

As we grew, so did our family of pets. Along with a dog and cat, we now had two canaries, a parakeet, a tiny turtle, an ant farm, and a small fish tank. Mom took care of the canaries and fish bowl, we girls cared for the rest. Besides the responsibility of minding the menagerie, we also studied their traits.

We learned that turtles lay eggs and their shells are their skeletons. We'd watch Tom, our turtle, climb the plastic ramp of his enclosure to eat lettuce and hamburger before sunning himself under a fake, green palm tree. We studied ants that roamed in the sand through two plates of glass. And we watched the fish scurry after each other, racing to the water's top for food, and sometimes flipping over and dying. Soon to be taken to the toilet and flushed to Peter Pan's "Neverland."

That summer we anxiously awaited our vacation to Cape Cod. Dad packed the car with five suitcases, three pillows, six sheets and blankets, five beach towels, a birdcage, a turtle, a fishbowl, and Shiro, our white, long-haired cat. Gail sat in the middle between Mom and Dad. Virginia and I spread out in the back seat with Lucky between us.

On our way from town, Dad stopped at a filling station and had the oil and tires checked, the tank filled with gasoline, and the windows washed. All by a slicked-back, brown-haired teenager, wearing blue jeans and a white tee-shirt with a pack of cigarettes coiled into his sleeve. Mom requested maps of Massachusetts and Rhode Island. Being a lover of mathematics, she liked to figure out the time and distance of our journey as we traveled to the Cape.

Along the Boston Post Road, past Norwalk, we lowered our windows, cooling the Chevy, smelling diesel as we passed interstate trucks. Cylinder vehicles hauling gasoline. Vegetables nestled beneath canvas tarps. A yellow Mayflower moving van. Virginia stuck her arm out the window and pumped it up and down. Her elbow bent and her fist closed. The truck responded. Honk! Honk! She turned and waved, smiling at the driver's gesture.

We played games during the six-hour drive. "I spy with my little eye." And we checked license plates to see how many states we could list.

Then we sang songs: "By the Light of the Silvery Moon, I want to spoon, to my honey I'll croon love's tune." Or another chosen melody, "I'm Looking Over a Four-Leaf Clover." And still an extra special song from our parent's repertoire: "You are My Sunshine, my Only Sunshine."

Mom knew the lyrics to these old tunes but her off-key vocals kept us giggling in the backseat. Dad, wearing a pork pie hat as he drove, had a beautiful voice.

"Are we there yet?" Virginia asked.

Mom unfolded a map of Massachusetts and checked our position and our destination.

"It's less than an hour," she said. "We'll stop at the White Rabbit first."

As we came closer, Dad stuck his arm out the window to signal we were turning right, bent at the elbow, his hand pointed up. We always stopped at the White Rabbit Tea Room in Buzzard's Bay. It was Dad's favorite restaurant on our journey. We threaded our way through the gift shop to the dining room, staring at souvenirs, especially the bright orange starfish. How pretty they looked. *Boy, would that be neat to have one on my dresser back home?*

After the hostess showed us to a table, a waitress arrived wearing a white dress with a blue-plaid apron, a pencil stuck behind her ear. Dad ordered clam chowder, supplemented with a bowl of oyster crackers. We followed his lead. Milk and cream, diced potatoes and celery, a little bacon, and gobs of clams.

After we left the White Rabbit and crossed the canal, we officially arrived on the Cape. Immediately the landscape changed. Sandy soil and rows of scrawny dwarf pines bracketed the three-lane highway, the middle lane used only for passing.

Water surrounded Scraggy Neck, our destination. Its link to the Cape peninsula was a causeway, a thin spit of land. At high tide, the sea crept over the link, still passable without any problems. At a super high tide, Scraggy Neck became an island and we couldn't cross. We turned onto the narrow gravel road that stretched over the estuary and continued past yellowing fields and sun-bleached cedar cabins, dust billowing behind our Chevy.

"There's the water tower," Virginia shouted, pointing to the cream-colored base, jutting thirty feet into the air.

When we arrived at the wood-sided cottage, insect remnants had thoroughly smeared the front of the car.

While Dad cleaned the grill and windshield, we brought our luggage inside. Mom carried the birdcage into their bedroom and turned to help the three of us make our beds on the loveseat and couch in the living room. Shiro and Lucky immediately began to explore their surroundings, both inside and out.

Now that we had settled in, Virginia was the first to climb the water tower. It seemed to be our rite of passage. Then it was my turn, then Gail's. Cirrus clouds, wispy and white, high in the sky seemed to smile at us as we ambled around the twenty-foot-high, narrow platform.

"Okay. That's enough!" Dad yelled, raising his hand over his brow to stare up at us. "Let's get to the beach."

We scrambled from the tower and raced into the cabin to change into bathing suits and gather some beach towels. We claimed our customary spots, Virginia and me in the backseat, Gail up front. Mom placed Lucky and Shiro inside the cabin, making sure the bedroom door was shut and the birdcage safe.

When we arrived at the beach, a small enclosed stretch of sand on the southside of Scraggy Neck, bands of seagulls soared overhead. They swooped down to feed on surfacing fish, splashing into Buzzards Bay and rising again with the wind. Waves blew over the water, splattering the shore with countless whitecaps, foaming and lapping at the sand. Perfect for body surfing.

Once our towels were spread on the beach, we raced into the water. Standing waist deep, my sisters and I turned and watched the incoming waves. As they approached, we pointed our hands toward land and pushed off, riding the waves facedown as we neared the shore.

Before the afternoon ended, Dad folded himself in a low crouch, bent down and hoisted each daughter individually to his shoulders. We dove out from the high perch, into the warm waters of the Bay.

This was one of the few times we really bonded with our father. As a commuter into New York City, he was gone most of the workday. His weekends were spent doing chores around the house, playing tennis, or socializing with adult friends. Our time on the Cape allowed us to have his undivided attention and to truly connect with him: his humor, his ethics, and his values.

Every day at the Cape was spent swimming and exploring. Mom took us on nature walks, identifying birds and wildflowers along the paths. Bright yellow goldenrod, orange trumpet creepers, and pink lady slippers. Following the shore were sandpipers and terns and high in the meadows were chickadees, jays, and finches. Remnants of a large mansion, with only its foundation still visible, was within walking distance of our cottage. Years ago, it had been destroyed by fire. Only a few brick chimneys and the stone foundation walls, a skeleton of the building, were visible. The turn-of-the-century estate had been left to disintegrate.

The best time on the Cape, however, was spent at the beach. We waded in warm waters and swam in undulating waves, approaching at a steady flow, streaming toward shore. We collected pink shells and tiny blue pieces of glass with rounded edges, polished by the sand and the constant waves of the sea. Sand lined our pockets, filled with pretty shells and sea glass, all to be brought back to the cottage. When washed, we added them to a glass lamp base, a reminder of another fantastic summer vacation.

On the last night on the Cape this particular summer, Mom and Dad joined our Darien neighbors for an afternoon and evening in Chatham, shopping and enjoying a fancy dinner at a seaside restaurant. We were old enough to stay at the cottage by ourselves.

While exploring, Virginia borrowed a rowboat from one of our neighbors, one that was tied near the causeway. When floating the boat close to shore, we gathered starfish from the sandy bottom. The ones we had seen, but could not afford, in the local gift shops. We found several starfish, sandy colored with squirming hydraulic feet beneath their five arms. We held onto the boat's gunnels and delicately placed the starfish in the bottom. Afterwards, the boat was reattached to its anchored pole and we returned to our cabin, walking along a sandy trail past the dunes.

In the kitchen Virginia reached under the counter and brought out a lobster pot. She filled it with water and turned on the stove. When bubbles rose in a steady stream, she carefully dumped the starfish into the boiling water. Gail scrutinized the procedure, standing on her tiptoes as she looked into the container. The starfish immediately turned bright orange and curled into a ball, not anything like the stretched-out souvenirs in the gift shops. Just then the cabin door creaked open.

"What's that smell?" Mom said when she walked through a gauntlet of rancid odor. "Something stinks!"

"What's burning?" Dad asked.

"We were going to surprise you," Virginia said as she stood by the stove, twirling a large wooden spoon through the boiling water. "We caught some starfish and were going to make gifts. Presents for you."

The acrid smell of cooking starfish, putrid and reeking, overwhelmed the cottage. Steam spread upward from the pot, penetrating the walls and ceiling, sweeping the sour smell throughout the rooms, soaking the curtains over the sink.

"Open the windows," Mom said, her jaw clenched. "Gail, take this towel and swish it around. Barbara, make sure the window screens are down. Virginia, step aside. Dad will throw the pot outside."

She issued a string of commands like a field marshal in the middle of a battle. Dad hurled the water and starfish twenty feet from the cabin, onto the sandy ground and left the stinking pot outside, upside down. He took a large spoon and dug a hole to bury the starfish, obliterating the stench. Inside was another matter. With all of us completing Mom's instructions, the smell dissipated, but just barely. When it was time to go to bed, we buried our heads under sheets, the pungent odor, like rotting meat, still clung to our blankets. Eventually, we fell asleep. On our last night at Scraggy Neck during that particular summer vacation in 1952.

# FIREFLIES

Outside, night was closing in, drawing the warmth from a surprisingly hot autumn day. In the thick timbers behind Mrs. Louis' house, branches and stickers grasped my clothes as I walked to Robbie's house. I detested the walk in the woods, afraid of the darkness, afraid of being tangled with briars. But I wanted a playmate to help catch fireflies. Susan, one of my best friends, had moved away. I had no one to help me catch fireflies but Robbie. The sun had receded behind the fir and leafless maple trees and the fireflies rose to take its place. Phosphorous yellow lights danced in the wind as the male firefly attempted to attract a female, blinking on and off with a mating beacon.

Robbie joined me in his backyard, catching the shining insects and trapping them in glass Mason jars. We each had about fifteen fireflies, pulsating colorful lights. When I returned home, Dad took his wooden-handled ice pick and jabbed holes in the metal top.

That night in bed on my stomach, I tried to read a Nancy Drew book by firefly light. It didn't work. Better to turn on the bedside lamp. My bedroom disappeared as I joined Nancy on her quest to solve the latest mystery. The fireflies continued to pulsate, remaining until morning when I released them from the jar.

# PLAYING "STICK"

As hot summer heat filled the days, Virginia and I rode our black, three-speed bicycles to the Noroton Bay Beach Club. Each of us had a bathing suit wrapped in a towel on a rack above the rear tire. In front next to our silver bells, we dangled lunch pails filled with a sandwich, an apple, and a drink in a thermos.

We smelled low tide, mud and seaweed as we parked our bikes near the rock wall entrance. After entering separate changing rooms, we put on bathing suits and sauntered to the end of the slender jetty, high above the water. Out in Long Island Sound, a single white sail bent into the wind. I stood for a moment watching it, my hand cupped over my brows, sheltering my eyes from the sun.

We draped towels on gray-painted Adirondack chairs, covering our clothes and lunch, and ambled down the angled plank to the floating dock. Jan, Johnny, Tom, and Robbie stood with their backs to us, staring at the water, waiting for a popsicle stick to emerge. I leaned over to watch. As soon as I saw the slender object rising to the water's surface, I jumped into a tangle of splashing kids. I grabbed the stick, holding it high for everyone to see. As I swam back, Robbie, still on the dock, tucked his body, his knees to his chest, and bombarded me with a cannonball.

We played "stick" for hours, with one person taking a popsicle stick and diving into the water. Maybe shoving it in the mud. Thereby giving the diver enough time to climb back on the dock and possibly retrieve the stick again. Nearby wooden pilings girdled the pier, allowing us to swim and still be safe. Dark shadows under the jetty hid the crossbeams encrusted with muscles and sharp barnacles.

Afterward, five of us sat at the top of the wharf and ate our sandwiches. Jan walked home for lunch as she lived across the street. When she returned, we were lying on towels, soaking up rays, toasting one side and then the other, taking our compulsory thirty-minute nap after lunch. A seagull perched on a piling, waiting for a discarded bread crust to be thrown its way. When the Johnston siblings, Jane and Ginny, joined us for another round of stick, the gull startled and flew away, wheeling out into the bay.

Eventually, a few quit playing. They wanted to dive. First from the board on the floating dock and then off the high board at the top of the pier. Squinting in the noonday sun, I watched swan dives and backflips, tucks and pikes, somersaults and jackknives. Displaying new tricks and skills. Tom was one of the best and showed everyone, even Gary, the new lifeguard, how to maneuver the aerial twists. Dave and Prim, the regular lifeguards, followed his examples.

Grabbing our towels, Jan and I left to explore the beach, tiptoeing across the scorching sand. I raced to the water with Jan right beside me. Ribbons of wet sand squelched beneath our toes and cooled our feet. We walked head down, looking for unusual shells tangled in seaweed.

As the waves washed over rocks, creamy foam formed on the sand. The two of us explored several tidal eddies, our fingers in the waters finding sea snails sucking their heads into their shells, blueish barnacles attached to fallen branches, and hermit crabs moving in stolen shells.

Gulls, white against the dark blue sky, flew overhead, braying like donkeys, and landing on houses and telephone poles. We walked past a stranded jellyfish at the mercy of the currents, unmoved by its predicament. I hated them, afraid of being stung. Huge strands of seaweed littered the sand. Scattered in scalloped lines. We squished the puffy bubbles and listened to them pop.

As the day waned, we returned to the changing rooms and joined Virginia in the shower corridor. We watched her pull the metal chain and shiver as the cold water splashed over her body. I was next. I hated the routine. Our parents required us to rinse off before changing into our clothes. The freshwater was always cold, freezing cold.

# JUNIOR HIGH
## 1954 - 1958

# DOCTOR ROSS

Gail often fished from the Noroton Bay pier, at least twice a week during the summer. She rode her bike, carrying an assortment of fishing gear to the jetty, along with her lunch so she could enjoy a full day of fishing. Any fish she caught in the bay, usually flounders, would be placed in a water-filled bucket, before being transferred to the wicker basket in front of her handlebars and brought home for dinner. Using bait, she cast into the bay, over and over again.

On one of her casts, she accidentally snagged her arm. The metal hook rammed in deep, past the barb. There was no way she could get it out. She cut the line and gathered her gear. Since her arm didn't hurt, she didn't tell anyone and mounted her bike. Gail positioned the pole on her side and pedaled up Nearwater Lane to Woodland Drive, over a mile away and all uphill.

"Look what happened," Gail said as she walked into the house.

Mom took one look and said, "Let me get it out." She washed Gail's arm with brown soap and took a pair of pliers from Dad's tool kit. Barely touching the hook, she attempted a slight twist.

"That hurts, Mom!" Gail yelled.

"What's happening?" Dad said when he heard the noise in the kitchen. "You can't get that out, Florence. It's too deep. Call Dr. Ross and I'll drive her to his office."

"Can I go?" I asked.

"Sure. We'll take the Crosley."

The three of us piled in. Gail sat in the front seat, looking casually over the dashboard, her arm in her lap. She didn't seem worried. Dad, however, was obviously anxious and floored the Crosley, overtaking cars and trucks. I sat in the backseat, watching houses whip by, curious as to Gail's upcoming procedure.

We arrived at Dr. Ross's office and were immediately ushered into his exam room. On top of Gail's right arm just below the elbow, a fish hook was deeply embedded, the barb protruding outward. Dad helped her climb on the examining table while a nurse waited nearby. When Dr. Ross entered the room, wearing a white jacket, I noted his thick black hair, slicked back and shining with pomade. He asked Gail to open her mouth and stuck a wide tongue depressor inside. Leaning over, he took her pulse while staring at his watch. Next, he unwrapped his stethoscope from around his thick neck and listened to Gail's heart and lungs. Dad and I watched the proceedings while the nurse left to take care of another patient. Dr. Ross rubbed a disinfectant on her skin around the hook and added a numbing solution. He knocked off the barb with black mini pliers, and with his fingers skimming over Gail's skin, he slowly withdrew the metal hook. Gail's face showed no concern; she was surprisingly calm throughout his probing. That is, until he asked her to lower her shorts and came toward her, flicking a syringe in front of his face.

"No, you don't!" She screamed.

Gail jumped off the examining table and raced around the room. I held out my arms but she passed right under them. After her second time scurrying past us, Dad finally caught hold and steadied her. Dr. Ross, puffing and overweight, came at her and stabbed the needle into her butt. I thought Gail was going to die. Her screams and howls filled the room. I cupped my hands over my ears and turned away.

"That was a tetanus shot. It'll stop any infection, specifically lockjaw," Dr. Ross said. "But in this case, a locked jaw might be desired," he said smiling at my father. This was my only time seeing Dr. Ross laugh. He was a strict, by-the-book, type of man. You went into his exam room, Dr. Ross saw you, and you left. No chatting, no joking.

Gail gave him an ugly look, scrunching her face and rubbing her bottom. The three of us walked from the office to the Crosley, parked in the shade, and climbed inside. Dad had left the windows open and the keys in the ignition. Typical of small-town freedoms in the fifties, he was unconcerned about any possible misdemeanors.

"Wash up. Dinner will be ready in a few minutes," Mom said when we arrived home.

While we ate, Mom and Virginia asked questions, wanting to hear all the details of the visit with Dr. Ross. Our dinner time was more than a place for shared meals. My parents would dole out family wisdom and quiz us on our opinions. Dr. Ross was our family physician and the go-to doctor for almost anything we needed. Dad and I related the issue of screaming and running around the examining table. Everyone laughed, including Gail. Then Dad became serious.

"It's amazing. Dr. Ross takes care of half the families in Darien. He saves us from illness and death and yet he's not allowed to join the country club."

"Why not?" Virginia asked.

"I think it's because he's Jewish. What do you think, Florence?"

"The country club is pretty strict from what I've heard. No Jews or coloreds. We don't have people of color in town unless they're servants. They couldn't afford the country club anyway so that's not an issue. As for Jews, the country club is private so I guess they can choose whoever they want as members."

"I think that's terrible," I said.

# HURRICANE CAROL

Out in the Atlantic Ocean, somewhere near the Bahamas, great sheets of rain gathered and drifted up the coast from Florida to New England. By late August 1954, a warm wind hurled across Darien, strong and gusting stronger. Clouds jostled against each other, crashing and marching from the Sound. The weather turned ugly and menacing, preparing for the upcoming storm. Treetops bent together and clouds darkened, leaves turned coal black.

Rain and wind made the outside cold, and for the second day in a row, we stayed inside. Under pewter skies, Virginia, Gail, and I played Pick-up Sticks, Chinese Checkers, and Monopoly. Sitting on the living room carpet, we heard tree branches scraping against the side of the house. Windowpanes rattled in their frames. Leaves flew everywhere. On lawns. On roads. On houses. With distant grumbling of thunder, lightning sliced across the horizon and torrential rains escaped from the sky. Lucky dashed upstairs and hid under Virginia's bed, curling into a tight ball, his feet wrapped under his body. He would not emerge until dinner.

Hurricane Carol had arrived. It was the first recorded Category 5 hurricane and was the most powerful storm to strike Southern New England since the 1938 Hurricane. Schools closed as strong gusts battered cars and buildings. Streetlights shuddered in the extreme wind, the driving rain falling at a slant, almost horizontally, slashing against our windows, snapping limbs and knocking trees into powerlines. A massive tree had ripped from the ground, its roots looking like tendrils spiraling into the air. We lost electricity.

From the fireplace mantle, Mom retrieved the sterling-based, hurricane lamps she had received as wedding presents. She lit the candles and watched them glitter inside the glass cylinders. The flames reflected her anxiety, fear showed in her face.

The storm continued to rage. A lashing wind whipped at our house. The garage doors soared from their frames, bouncing over our driveway and slamming onto nearby bushes. Cascades of rainwater fell into our window wells, sliding through their casings, creeping into the basement. Two feet of water flooded our cellar. The heavy rain ripped at trees, streets, and houses. Everything outside was battered and soaked.

The storm rinsed the sky, bringing everything into bright focus the following morning. Deep impressions of horse hooves scalloped the grass in our backyard. Loose horses from the Franklin's farm roamed the area and trampled across neighborhood lawns and fields.

When the wind had decreased and the rain had diminished, Dad joined a group of men at the Noroton Fire Department. They were all volunteers and left immediately to help people in the flooded section of Noroton Bay. The Long Island Sound heaved gusting waves against the shore and over stone walls, splashing and rumbling, covering the low-lying streets with four feet of water. In all directions, cars and boats were destroyed, houses damaged, and trees demolished. Half-submerged sailboats drifted away from their moorings. In the distance the firemen heard the muffled roar of the sea.

The volunteers traveled by boat, up and down the roads, rescuing people trapped in their homes. Dad watched one woman attempting to exit a second-floor window right below a peak in her roof. Power lines extended from the eave to a nearby pole.

"Don't touch them!" Dad yelled. "Go to the stairs. We'll save you."

Dad and another firefighter climbed from the boat and walked through almost waist-deep water to the entrance steps. With a lot of pulling, they wedged the front door open, just wide enough for the woman to slip through. She was soaking wet when Dad helped her over the gunnels and into the boat; the other volunteers quickly wrapped her in a blanket and maneuvered the boat to the firetruck, parked at the Noroton Bay stone pillars. A firefighter helped her from the boat and carried her to the truck. Someone handed her a hot cup of coffee and she sat in the truck, shivering and waiting.

Once their jobs were completed and the rescued people were brought to the station, the volunteer firefighters returned to their own homes to repair and replace. With electricity back on, Dad telephoned to have new garage doors installed. He borrowed a pump, and for the next few hours, he drew water from the basement. Meanwhile, Virginia towed a dirt-stuffed wagon to the backyard. Gail and I took trowels and the three of us filled all the hoof holes throughout the lawn.

# JUNIOR HIGH CLASSES

Nervous enthusiasm escaped us during the first morning of school as we poured from buses at the Junior High's building. Children from all Darien elementary schools joined the crowd of students in the auditorium. We were assigned homerooms and lockers, instructed about specific subjects, and the ringing of bells. Instead of being in one classroom for the entire day, as we had in elementary school, we were told to change rooms whenever we heard a bell sound. All new procedures and very exciting.

When the noon bell rang, chattering students filled the hallways on their way to the lunchroom. After a quick meal, we spilled out the double doors to the playground. With no need to be silent, we could now socialize. We talked about summer excursions and compared black and white photos taken in photo booths. Inserting a quarter, sitting on a bench, and gawking at a camera. When we pulled the curtain shut, we made faces or smiled at the camera. A moment later, four pictures appeared from a little slot.

The girls pretended not to notice the boys who were noticing them as we leaned against the brick building and talked about our vacations. Junior sailors from the Noroton Yacht Club competed in dinghy races, sailing every Saturday. Susie, a friend from when we were toddlers at Noroton Bay, was one of the better sailors and told us of her recent trophies. Others mentioned New England camps, exotic trips to the Rocky Mountains, and horseback riding competitions.

---

Early one February morning, when the sun hugged the treetops and cold air cascaded from Canada, the radiators began noisily clunking as steam surged through their pipes. In my bedroom with the door shut behind me, I opened my window and listened to the sounds as the wind whistled over rooftops and trees. Taking the satin hem of my wool blanket and hauling it past my shoulders, I snuggled back under the covers and waited until my alarm clock sounded. Seven a.m. Time to get ready for school.

I wore a wool skirt, white blouse, and a plaid vest and hurried downstairs for breakfast. Sporting a camel-haired coat with a long scarf wrapped around my collar, I gathered my books and joined the other girls walking to the bus stop on Nearwater Lane. We chatted as we strolled, catching up on the latest news and popular records. Bill Haley and The Comets had just released "Rock Around the Clock." We sang as we walked, shrill and loud.

*One, two, three o'clock, four o'clock rock.*

*Five, six, seven o'clock, eight o'clock rock.*

*Nine, ten, eleven o'clock, twelve o'clock rock.*

*We're going to rock around the clock tonight!*

Singing and swaying, all to the beat of our voices as we strolled up Woodland Drive.

My favorite class in Junior High was with Mr. Holahan, a short and stocky teacher filled with energy. He brought mathematics to life by using everyday problems and baseball statistics as teaching tools.

"Stan Musial's record for hits in a season is 299. If you have 200 hits with 42 games to go, how many hits do you need per game to break his record?"

Ken, an outstanding football player, sat in front of me, both of us on the aisle near the inside wall, facing the front of the classroom. I stared at his flannel shirt and broad shoulders, wondering if he liked me. He was a good athlete, friendly to everyone, and well respected.

Mr. Holahan paced in front of the chalkboard and rapped the tip of his ruler against a desk to get our attention. With his overzealous enthusiasm, he periodically threw blackboard erasers around the classroom. I looked up as he stalked the rows of desks in front of large vertical windows, tapping shoulders, making sure his students were correctly solving problems. When he came to my side of the classroom, he knocked the top of Ken's head with closed knuckles. His forehead wrinkles sharpened as he stared down at Ken. I bit the end of my eraser, noticing Ken stare up at Mr. Holahan, watching a confrontation escalate. More agitated breaths between the two of them. Veins standing out on their necks. Just as Mr. Holahan was about to wrap Ken's head again, Ken jumped to his feet.

He had had enough! Ken grabbed Mr. Holahan's jacket, lifting him by his lapels and slamming him against the wall. I was stunned! My eyes wide open, my mouth agape. Puffing and panting with emotion and exertion,

Ken knew what was coming. He turned away, marching to the door and left the classroom, trudging directly to the principal's office.

He had a "Who do you think you are?" lecture. With no prior record, no attacks or fights of any kind, he got off lightly with only a weeklong detention.

Meanwhile Mr. Holahan, pale and speechless, stood with his back to the wall, shocked. After a moment's silence, he walked back to the chalkboard, obviously shaken, and gave us another problem to solve.

# THE HAUNTED HOUSE

A warm October wind swept across Darien. Virginia now in ninth grade and I in seventh. After Saturday's lunch Virginia and I played Monopoly on the living room floor. Rolling dice, advancing metal figures, and exchanging money. When the contest came to a close, we debated our next game.

"Let's explore," Virginia suggested.

"Okay. Where to?"

"Let's get Jane and Robbie. They'll want to come."

"Hey, Mom. We're going exploring," Virginia called as we walked out the backdoor.

"Okay. Be home in time for dinner."

We tramped over a well-worn path through the field across from our house, its sunburnt grasses interspersed with Queen Anne's lace, their tiny white blossoms stretching to our shins. When we arrived at the Johnston's back porch, Virginia opened the screen door and knocked on their kitchen door. Clouds of flies banged against the screen, trying to reach the inside before winter arrived.

"We're going exploring. Want to come?" Virginia asked the two blond siblings. All of us were dressed in the uniform of the day, dungarees and tee shirts with white sneakers.

"Sure. I'll bring a flashlight," Jane said.

"Should I bring anything?" her brother asked.

"No. Let's go."

"I want to come, too," said Ginny, their younger sister.

"Okay. But you have to mind us," Jane instructed.

The five of us went down the porch steps, across their backyard, and climbed the bordering stone wall. Passing the infamous stump, we trekked through the remaining woods, and into a cut field of harvested hay. Not baled but mowed and left to dry. From there we tramped to Nearwater Lane.

On the narrow, uneven sidewalk along the main road to the beach, we marched single file until we came to a large, imposing old house with a small caretaker's cottage positioned beside it. The house, an impressive, two-story wooden structure, had been built as a summer home for wealthy New Yorkers during the turn of the century. It now stood empty and desolate. As we planted ourselves on the road, staring at the structure, a web of dark shadows sliced across the expansive lawn. The tall windows along the main floor reflected slashing rays of an afternoon sun, the dark upper windows seemed to glare at us.

"Let's try to get inside," Virginia said.

A rusted iron fence in need of cleaning and new paint surrounded the property. Virginia pushed open the squeaking metal gate. We followed her up the front steps. At the eloquent, paneled door she pressed the thumb latch on the brass handle. Nothing happened. The door didn't budge. It was firmly locked.

"Let's see if anything's open."

Walking around the side of the house, we noticed a small basement window slightly ajar. Nudging it inward, Robbie crawled through the opening and dropped to the cement floor. One by one, we trailed him into the damp and dingy basement. The foundation walls were formed of large rocks, hauled in by teams of horses, typical of houses built in that era. We smelled a damp, musty odor and heard mice scurrying in the dark abyss. Jane used her flashlight to scan the room, casting us in alternating pools of light and dark, glare and shadow. Cobwebs and dust engulfed the overhead pipes and rafters. We navigated between empty bookcases and overflowing storage boxes toward a narrow staircase. Holding onto the rough-hewed railing, we sneaked up the stairs.

Once on the main floor, Jane turned off her flashlight. Sunlight filtered in through vertical windows and I breathed a sigh of relief. We meandered from room to room, most of them empty except for a few pieces of furniture covered with white sheets. The walls were littered with cracks, the oak floors showed years of wear, and layers of paint peeled from cream-colored baseboards. Positioned near the doors were push-button electric switches.

Thick, velvet curtains hung limply around each window and layers of dust covered the sills. Under one of the front windows, Virginia discovered a window seat and opened its lid. Inside were pages and pages of sheet music.

"They probably had a grand piano here," she said as she swept her hand around the room. "Look at all the music pages and look at this old songbook."

We joined her next to the window and glanced into the bench, full of scents of faded grandeur, distant reminders of an elegant past. I imagined a formal recital of classical music being played at the piano. Women in colorful evening gowns and men in black dinner jackets positioning themselves on chairs and window seats, all decorated with heavily brocaded cushions.

From the front parlor, we continued into the kitchen. A water spot stained the sagging ceiling and dripping faucets discolored the double sinks. A butler's pantry stood bare of plates and glasses. No silver goblets. No crystal snifters. No champagne flutes.

After we had thoroughly inspected the downstairs, Virginia led the way up the wide staircase to the second floor. In the bathroom, we spotted a white porcelain tub with brass feet. Next to it stood a toilet bowl with a dark stain where the water had drained away. An oak box near the ceiling had a brass chain hanging from the wooden container.

"What's that?" Ginny asked.

"Everyone knows that," her brother said. "The box is filled with water and when you pull the chain, the toilet flushes."

"Okay, smarty pants. What's this?" Ginny asked as she opened a door to the linen closet.

He had no idea but his older sister did. Jane stepped forward and showed us how it worked.

"It's a clothespress. You fold your sheets and put them inside the closet. Then you turn this knob and that large board comes down and presses against the sheets," Jane said as she pointed to the metal sphere. "You keep turning until the board is tight against the sheets. Everything comes out neat and pressed. No need for ironing."

Jane probably learned that fact from her mother who loved antiques. Besides decorating with vintage furniture, Mrs. Johnston used a treadle sewing machine to make her girls' clothes. And she wrote letters and reports on an old Remington typewriter.

A large bedroom in the front corner of the impressive house revealed a turret, a tower protruding from the main structure. Several small windows encircled the tiny room; its ceiling rising on all sides toward the peak. I envisioned an upholstered chair with a shaded lamp on a little table. A cozy space, perfect for reading.

On an interior wall of the bedroom, Virginia opened a door to a large, walk-in closet. Jane clicked on her flashlight and we followed her into the dark, rectangular space. The door creaked shut as Robbie pulled the glass knob and turned to find everyone sitting on the floor, cross-legged or hugging knees to their chests. Jane placed her light in the middle, its reflection bouncing across our faces and casting eerie shadows on the walls. Robbie sat on the floor and Virginia began her ghost stories. She looked around, clearly enjoying herself. Her voice lowered and quivered as she spun her sinister tales. Time passed as we listened to story after story, the gist of each being an ugly man who lurked inside a haunted house, turning on lights unexpectedly, playing a piano at all hours of the night, and screaming at innocent children who lived there with their elderly parents.

Hearing scraping sounds from beyond the closet walls, I felt uneasy. *Was there someone else in the house?*

Just then a thud sounded above us. It must have originated in the attic. We looked at each other. *What was that?* We rose and scampered from the closet. No one wanted to listen to any more ghost stories. They seemed too real. Too close.

As we hurried down the hall toward the staircase, Jane paused. She was the oldest of the five and showed little fear. Still curious, she opened another door. Her younger sister, Ginny, started to go through the opening. Virginia stuck out her arm and Ginny abruptly stopped, staring at my sister. The door led to a dumb waiter and the contraption was stationed in the basement, the place where large washing tubs now stood empty. Ginny would have fallen two flights if she hadn't been blocked. Fortunately, Virginia had noticed the frayed ropes. She thought they might have rotted after so many years of neglect. For me, even with the beginning of darkness, I could see the empty cubicle in the house's freight elevator.

We left the second floor and went immediately to the foyer. An ash-gray shadow brushed against the dining room wall. And then it vanished. *Did I actually see something?* I thought as I nudged Ginny to the side. She jumped at my touch. We were both nervous and frightened.

It was time to go. We gathered around the front door. No one wanted to escape through the basement. Virginia turned the deadbolt and we dashed outside. Daylight had faded to a chilling dusk. We rushed through the metal gate, letting it clang behind us.

"What's going on?" a man shouted from the caretaker's yard. "Get out of here!"

We raced up the narrow sidewalk along Nearwater Lane. A shot rang out. We heard leaves and branches breaking overhead. Bullets ripped through treetops, shattering the crowns of oaks and elms. I was breathing hard, my heart banging in my chest. Under a sentry of trees, I flew over fallen leaves, leaves in somber shades of beige and brown, and finally stopped. I hunched over, my hands on my knees, and gulped air, catching my breath. We smiled, then chuckled, and finally howled with laughter. With disbelief, with gratitude, and with infectious joy. Uncontrollable and with complete abandon.

"Did he really shoot at us?" I asked, stifling a giggle.

"Yea, but he aimed high," Jane said. "He just wanted to scare us."

"Well, he certainly scared me," I said.

Robby relieved himself behind a withering ash, gnarled and furred with moss, before rejoining our group. We jogged up Nearwater Lane, once again in single file. Not a car passed in either direction. Turning left on Woodland, the five of us marched the rest of the way down the slight hill toward our homes as an ebony night enveloped the street.

"Don't tell!" Virginia yelled. We waved to the Johnston siblings and slipped into our kitchen, just before dinner.

# TONY, THE GOOSE

It was early morning, 1954. Sunlight sparkled off newly leafed trees and tulips began to sprout. Easter was right around the corner when Mom surprised us with three ducklings and a gosling. The waterfowl babies, crowded inside a cardboard box, tan and fluffy in their down coats, quacked incessantly. Mom carried the box to our backyard and gently spilled the babies onto the lawn. We surrounded the noisy birds, staring in disbelief, peppering Mom with questions.

"Are they ours?"

"Where're they from?"

"Can we play with them?"

Virginia named the ducklings, Andy, Brandy, and Candy. I named the gray gosling, Tony. He was my favorite. I fed and talked to him, cradled him in my lap and petted his fluffy feathers. We bonded instantly, imprinting as it's called. He followed me everywhere. When I played croquet, he waddled right beside me, shadowing my every step. When I paused to contemplate a stroke, lining my mallet with the ball, he stopped and started plucking at grass. He didn't move until I did.

The ducklings swam in our red metal wagon and Tony splashed in a large blue basin. We watched them slurp the water, raising their heads high to swallow. They provided chores as well as fun. Mom was pleased with our care of the little waterfowl babies. As they grew, one duckling fell behind. It looked weak. It didn't follow the others and soon lay down, never to move again. A few weeks later, there was only one duckling. Before long only Tony was left, none of the ducklings lived past six weeks. As he aged, his creamy down turned dark gray with white dabs. I cuddled my goose, stroked him, and taught him to come, handing him lettuce bits as his reward. Lucky stood beside Tony, begging for his own treat. But I had only lettuce.

As Tony would be all alone in the garage at night, I brought him inside and carried him to my bedroom. He slept on the top mattress of my wooden bunk bed. I had covered it with layers of newspapers. Geese are not easily housetrained, if at all. The bunk bed had side rails, foot and headboards. He couldn't escape. Lucky slept on the bottom mattress with me, curled at my feet. Lottie, my parakeet, was in his cage near my front window. Life was good.

Hearing noisy scratching just as the sun shone into my bedroom, I turned in my bed and looked up. A face appeared over the railing of the upper bunk. Tony! *Why was he up so early?* I ignored the sounds above me and disappeared under the covers. He'd just have to wait.

When it was time for school, I carried Tony downstairs and out the backdoor. He had his water and food waiting for him on the side of the garage. After I dressed, ate breakfast, and walked down the driveway, Tony followed right beside me, flapping his wings, snorting his disapproval of my fast pace.

Darn! I picked him up and carried him back to his fenced cage, a large wire enclosure Dad had created under the maple tree. When I returned each afternoon, Tony squawked a greeting, raising his head and honking for all to hear. I opened the wire gate and ran from him, calling his name. He raced after me, his wings flapping outward. He never flew, maybe he didn't know how since he had imprinted with me. I hugged and petted him, Lucky tried to get between us, sticking his nose next to my face, licking my cheek, wanting his own caresses.

During June, listless heat baked Darien and I took refuge at the Noroton Bay Beach Club. I jumped on my bike with a lunchbox on the handlebars and my bathing suit wrapped in a towel in the front basket. When I returned, Tony once again greeted me with hair-raising honks, letting the neighbors know I had returned. Our routine was the same, running about the backyard together, Lucky trying to overcome his rival. The two of them chasing after me, vying for my attention as I laughed at their antics.

Soon it was time for camp. The month of July at Hillsboro Girls Camp in New Hampshire. *What would happen to Tony?* Mom called Uncle Dick and asked if I could keep him at his place as he had some acreage and a large pond.

"Of course," he said. "When will you bring him?"

"How does Saturday sound? About nine," Mom said. "We'll continue to Barbara's camp afterward."

"Okay. See you then."

After we dropped Tony in Uncle Dick's backyard, near the pond, he waddled, as only geese can do. Stepping deliberately, placing one webbed foot in front of the other, his toes turned inward. He headed instantly toward the water and plunked in, paddling directly to the middle and raising his head, waving it up and down, as if to say "good-bye."

I joined Mom, Dad, Virginia, and Gail, and meandered back to the car, my head down, sad to leave my pet goose for the month.

There was no time to be depressed. At Hillsboro I joined my Darien friends for horseback riding, crafts, archery, canoeing, and swimming. I was on the dive team, part of the relay swim team, and the synchronized swim squad. With so many water activities, I was nicknamed, "Bubbles." I never liked "Barbara," it seemed so formal. That summer, many of us changed our names. Virginia became "Ginny" and I became "Bubbles." I couldn't wait to tell my parents.

They arrived two weeks later, sitting in a brand-new Cadillac convertible. Aunt Irene, Uncle Dick's new wife, drove the car onto the campgrounds with the top down. She and Mom wore scarfs tightly wrapped around their heads, trying to keep their hair in place. Everyone turned to see the shiny automobile park in front of the tennis courts. Sparkling white with a rich, red leather interior.

With a burst of enthusiasm, I told them about taking second place on a large bay horse; my swim team winning in the relay races; and being renamed "Bubbles." I said it all in one sentence, bouncing on the balls of my feet as I spilled the news.

"That's great, Barbara," Mom said.

"No, my name is Bubbles," I countered.

"That's fine and I'm sure everyone calls you that but I think your family will still call you Barbara," Mom said.

Dad and Uncle Dick laughed at my name change. I overheard them saying something about a secretary being called Bubbles and that she might be in for more than she bargained. Feeling disheartened, I was glad to see Ginny and Gail arriving with their own camp news.

"Why aren't the Boston girls going home?" I asked.

"There's a polio outbreak," Mom said. "They have to stay here until they can receive Dr. Salk's vaccine."

"When will that be?"

"Soon, I'm sure."

The seven of us walked around the campgrounds, showing off our cabins and the beautiful lake. After a while, the adults left for a late lunch in town before heading back to Darien.

On our drive home ten days later, I told them I had changed my name again. This time to "Bobbi."

"That's much better," Mom said. "We'll try to remember your new name but it might take a while."

"So, what's with Tony?" I asked.

Dead silence. Dad kept his eyes on the road and said, "You tell her."

"Tell me what?"

"There was an incident at Uncle Dick's," Mom said softly. "Tony died."

"What happened?" I said, tears forming in my eyes.

"Uncle Dick had him for dinner," Dad said, gripping the steering wheel, his voice low with anger. "And he invited us over!"

"Okay, Jim. That's enough," Mom said. "It was a mistake, I'm sure."

"Well, it might have been a mistake, but he didn't have to ask us to join them in their "gourmet" feast," Dad grumbled. "And you ate some of Tony. I didn't. Not even one bite!"

"I was only being polite," Mom responded. "You had such a good time at camp, Barbara. I'm sorry we brought you bad news."

Ginny put her arm around me and pulled me closer. She whispered, "We'll miss Tony but I bet Lucky is happier."

She looked into my brimming eyes and smiled. I smiled back and wiped tears from my cheeks. With pillows in the corners of the backseat, we rested our heads, soon falling fast asleep.

# BONFIRE ON RINGS END ROAD

Locally we called it cabbage night. To others, it was "mischief" night, the night before Halloween. A time to cause trouble but not to *get* into trouble. A full moon brightened the sky that evening, causing shadows from nearby trees to scatter across our neighbors' lawns. A scary time, perfect for soaping windows or toilet papering bushes.

Dad and Mr. Hall, our neighbor, had arranged to startle their good friend, Mr. Hazelton, who lived a few houses away on Woodland Drive. Taking an empty spool of thread, Dad notched the wooden ends and wound a string to the spool. With a pencil in the hollowed-out center, he placed the contraption on a window and pulled the string. Boom! It sounded like bullets smashing into a window. Mr. Hazelton came bellowing out the front door, running to the street, an abundance of swear words in his wake.

"Get the hell out of here!" he screamed into the darkness, shaking his fist toward the sky. He turned and stared at his footprints in the dirt, deep indentations in his newly seeded front lawn. "Damn you brats!"

Roaring laughter came from behind the bushes surrounding his sunroom windows. Mr. Hall and Dad showed themselves, causing Mr. Hazelton to cuss even more and even louder. Eventually, he calmed down and invited the two into the house. The three entered the house for drinks, Halloween stories, and more laughter.

While Dad played pranks in the neighborhood, I met Brenda and two other gals, all in their mid-teens, at the corner of Woodland and Nearwater. It was an unusually warm October night and we all wore Bermuda shorts. They chatted about their upcoming adventure for cabbage night. We cut through a pasture splashed with yellow black-eyed Susans, into some surrounding woods, and emerged on Rings End Road.

Pumpkins lined porch steps at the few houses dotting the paved street. No cars were left outside, they were all safely concealed in garages. We had no glass panes to soap. Television sets lit house windows with black and white forms and shaded table lamps shined out onto expansive lawns. The people inside were calm and peaceful. Too peaceful.

Brenda and her cronies, all at least a year older than me, decided to build a bonfire. I was happy to be included in this wild group of girls. We gathered sticks and a few small logs, forming a three-foot-high pile, right in the middle of Rings End Road. Building a nest of dry leaves at its base, one of the gals brought out some matches. She was a smoker and always had a book of matches along with a cigarette pack in her shirt pocket. She knelt before the mound of dry branches and struck a match to the leaves. A loud whoosh as flames gathered and engulfed the pile, sparks flying high into the air. We silently stood in a circle, staring at the fluorescent flames, flickering in the moonlight. Awed at the bright blaze, with its heavy smoke curling upward into the sky. Our faces bathed in the reflected flashes of fire. Fumes of oak and ash saturated the air.

As we stood watching the fire, listening to the crackle of burning branches, I heard the grim sounds of an approaching, but not yet visible, car. Soon the wail of sirens pierced the air, in the distance but coming closer. Someone had called the police.

"Run!" Brenda yelled.

And run we did, darting in all directions, away from the bonfire and into the nearby fields and forest. I snaked my way through the dark woods on the east side of the road, escaping from a potential police arrest.

As I stumbled through trees, moving into their dark shadows, I tumbled, head over heels, into a basement. Ruins of a historic house had appeared in my path, nothing left but its foundation, overgrown with weeds. I fell eight feet and crumbled onto a dirt floor. Rocks formed the foundation walls, leaves and muck covered the floor. The musty odor of damp dirt permeated the space. I heard pounding steps from an officer, his flashlight flaring overhead, its reflecting glow bounced off branches and their few remaining leaves. Shivering in the darkness, afraid of spiders and snakes, I remained a good ten inches from the rock wall, standing still with my arms wrapped around my body. I heard bare branches vibrating in the breeze above and the tread of the policeman.

"Come out," he yelled as he weaved his flashlight through the wedge of blackness. Back and forth. Back and forth.

I said nothing and stayed as still as possible, crouching now and hugging my knees. I listened to his footsteps, through the fallen leaves and twigs. And then there was silence. No more sounds. I waited until I heard cars pulling away, driving down Rings End Road.

Reaching up and placing a foot on a protruding stone, I struggled to pull myself out of the foundation. Slowly, I stumbled through the woods to the road. The drowned fire, its cold ash swept to the side. The police had vanished. The girls gathered in a circle, again at our site of mischief, laughing at the prank we had pulled.

"What happened to your leg?" Brenda asked as I limped toward her. I looked at my leg and saw blood oozing from my knee.

"You can't go home like that," she said. "Let's see if we can get some help."

A nearby house, a white vintage clapboard with a large front porch, had two carved pumpkins lighted as a welcome. Brenda knocked on the front door and we waited for someone to answer. An older man appeared, dressed in a Madras shirt with tan slacks, his feet tucked into brown loafers. He welcomed us inside. Surprisingly, he turned out to be a doctor. He took one look at my damaged leg and brought me into the living room and had me sit on a cushioned, straight back chair. In the background, I heard piano music, "Autumn Leaves," coming from his radio. Once my leg was cleaned with alcohol, he bandaged the wound and helped me to my feet.

"Why were you out tonight?" he asked.

Not wanting to be a snitch, Brenda answered, "Oh, we were just exploring when we heard the sirens. They scared us and we ran into the woods."

"So, you had nothing to do with the fire?" he said, smiling at her.

"Well, we didn't mean anything bad. We were just having a little fun," Brenda said. "You know it is 'cabbage night,' don't you?"

"I've heard that. Glad you're all safe and nothing terrible happened."

When he escorted us to the front porch, he told us his house had once been part of the Underground Railroad. It was considered a safe house, a depot. Previous owners had hidden escaping Negro slaves under the front porch until they could flee north on their path to freedom.

We all knew Darien was a historic town with English settlers residing since the 1600s. None of us knew it had been part of the Underground Railroad. Our night of adventure not only produced mischief-night hysteria but also a little history about helping slaves escape the South around the time of the Civil War.

# MRS. HALLIWELL'S DANCE CLASS

As the sun dipped in the sky, its last rays filtering through the trees, I joined other eighth-graders inside the First Congregational Church, in the alcove on the side of the sanctuary. I wore a pink party dress, its hem falling just below my knees, with two crinolines underneath, bouncing the skirt up and out. And a pair of stockings, each one attached to a garter belt surrounding my waist. All of us wore white gloves, even the boys in their dark suits with white shirts and skinny ties. The expected uniform for Mrs. Halliwell's dance class.

"Welcome, young ladies and gentlemen," Mrs. Halliwell said, standing in the center, swirling her hand around the room. She was a tiny woman and wore high, high heels. In her fingers she held a black metal clicker, something she used to get our attention. When she depressed the tongue, a "click" amplified throughout the space. We stopped and looked at her. This was the first day of dance class and we were learning her routine.

"From now on, I expect the ladies to sit against the windows and the gentlemen against the wall. Please move to your assigned areas."

We did as she asked. I noticed a few mothers peeking in the windows, watching their children in the dance class. The girls sat on one side of the room, the boys across the way, both groups politely facing each other, their hands in their laps while sitting on folding chairs.

Mrs. Halliwell showed the boys how to bow slightly when asking a girl to dance. And she demonstrated a small curtsy for the girls when we stood to accept the dance.

"Gentlemen, please walk to the lady of your choice and politely ask her to dance," Mrs. Halliwell instructed.

Some of the boys raced across the room but most awkwardly sauntered to one of the girls. *Please don't let me be the last to be picked*, I thought. Luckily, Jimmy asked me to dance and I was relieved of my anxiety. Poor Barbara, the tallest girl in our class, was the last to be chosen. Her dance partner was several inches shorter. The boys had not yet begun to grow. But grow they would. Soon to rise above the girls.

We danced in a large circle around the room, learning the box step, the foxtrot, the waltz. Whenever we heard the clicker, we changed partners. Sometimes my new dance partner towered over me. Sometimes his head fell below my chin. The girls walked backward. Twirling and swishing. Lots of "please" and "thank you" comments, all very formal and stilted. Mrs. Halliwell taught manners as well as dance steps.

I loved dressing up and learning to dance. Wednesday night was something to look forward to. We were allowed to wear lipstick but no other make-up. Before I entered the church building, I pinched my cheeks, bringing color to my face as I smiled at my friends coming into the class.

Some of the boys, however, were not as enamored with Mrs. Halliwell and her dance class. Hoby and Walt escaped through the windows one night, and Tom and Allan never even entered the building after their parents had left them at the church. An hour later, they were rounded up by the Darien police while walking beside the Post Road, strolling in their dark suits, still wearing their white gloves. After a brief lecture, they were unceremoniously delivered to their homes in Noroton Bay.

# GREENWICH COUNTRY CLUB

My house telephone rang in the hall. A stampede of feet raced to the phone with cries of, "I'll get it." I reached it first. Rusty Lambert, a classmate who lived on Nearwater Lane, was on the other end.

"Want to go to a dinner dance at the Greenwich Country Club? It's next Saturday."

"Sounds like fun. I've never been to a dinner dance. I'll ask my parents. Call me back in an hour."

For that matter, I had never even been on a date. My parents approved the dinner dance and Mr. Lambert collected me the following Saturday. Rusty and I sat in the backseat while his father drove. We talked about school activities but I didn't feel well. My orthodontist had just tightened my braces and my gums hurt. In my mind, I resembled an ugly duckling, wearing those hideous silver bands. Rusty sported a dark suit with a white shirt and navy tie. I wore a pale blue party dress with crinolines bunched underneath. We both wore white gloves. *What else?*

At the clubhouse, an impressive white building with black shutters, Rusty escorted me to its main entrance. He held out his elbow and I linked my arm into his. We both attended weekly dance classes with Mrs. Halliwell and accepted her protocol, glad to know what to do when we arrived.

Inside the foyer, we were directed to the dining room where all the other eighth-graders were taking their places at long, white-clothed tables. We eagerly anticipated a five-course dinner. That's what we had been told. There were more knives, forks, spoons, and goblets; more than I had ever seen at one setting. It was a relief to see other teens staring at the display on the table as we questioned which fork went with which course. Rusty pulled out a chair for me. He sat next to me and we watched the other teens to see what next was expected. A colored woman, wearing a white apron over a black dress, set a salad bowl in front of each of us. Rusty and I unfolded our napkins and placed them on our laps. *Take the outside fork first*, I remembered Mom telling me.

"I'm from New Jersey, but now I'm a New Englander," one of the girls said, attempting to start a conversation.

"Just because kittens are born in an oven, doesn't make them muffins," another girl said. That shut up everyone and we quietly continued eating, no one venturing into a new conversation.

When the salad was finished, I touched my lips with the napkin and looked across the table at a blond girl about my age. Smiling at each other, we watched as our plates were removed and the next course was started, tomato soup. While Rusty and I chatted, one of the boys bumped the table. His spoon clattered against the rim of the soup bowl. Heads turned to see what had happened. All of us were inspecting each other, scrutinizing everyone's move. So naïve, yet wanting to be accepted.

Following the soup was a fish dish and then the main course: chicken immersed in rich gravy, peas, and mashed potatoes. Taking my fork in my left hand, I gently pierced the chicken. I used my knife in my right hand to slice off a small section. I must not have had a good grip on the knife. It not only slid off the chicken but also skidded across my plate and propelled most of my peas onto the table.

"What happened?" Rusty asked as everyone at the table turned to inspect the stack of green globs on the sparkling white table cloth. My face must have been as red as the tomatoes in the salad. No one laughed. I felt the weight of everyone's eyes on me as they stared. Luckily the waitress arrived with a silver-backed brush and tiny dustpan. She immediately swept the mess from the table.

"Thank you," I said looking at her.

"You're fine," she whispered.

Let's get out of here," I hissed to Rusty.

"It's okay. They're not looking now. They're busy eating."

After my total embarrassment and the completion of the ceremonial dinner, we joined the other teens in the ballroom. Sitting hip to hip, Rusty and I inspected the couples, making comments to each other. Spurning rock 'n' roll, the tunes from the big bands of Tommy Dorsey and Glenn Miller permeated the air. Just conventional waltzes, swings, and foxtrots. They all wore white gloves and moved in shifting circles. Rusty and I merged with the dancers, perfecting our best steps from Mrs. Halliwell's class. No noise from a clicker. No swapping of partners. Just the musical sounds from the country club band.

# THE NICKERSON HOUSE

That following spring, Mr. Nickerson arrived at our backdoor early Saturday morning. As I stepped from our porch, the sun rose above the treetops, warming the day and sending bright slashes of rays through the budding leaves of spring. He had asked my mother if I could play with his granddaughter, to be her companion for the weekend.

"What's her rate for babysitting?" he had inquired a few days earlier.

"Fifty cents an hour," Mom replied.

"How about if I pay her $5 for Saturday and $3 for Sunday?"

"I think she'll be very pleased. What time will you be here on Saturday?"

"Eight o'clock. I'll take the girls downtown for breakfast. And I'll bring Barbara home in the late afternoon, around four."

"Barbara will be ready. Pick her up at our backdoor, on Woodland," Mom said. "Thanks for thinking of her. The girls will definitely have fun."

His ten-year-old granddaughter, Debby, sat in the front seat that Saturday and looked out the window at me. She wore a pretty blue dress and had her brown hair pulled back on each side with barrettes. When I opened the car door, she slid over and I introduced myself to her and to Mr. Nickerson. I also wore a dress, a yellow shirtwaist with a thin, navy leather belt. When I was inside and had shut the door, we drove to the Central Diner, near the Darien train station on the Boston Post Road. Its gray metal-framed building, long and narrow with large windows facing the street, reminded me of a passenger train car. At the diner Mr. Nickerson held the door open for Debby and me and we stepped inside, going right for the red-leather stools in front of the counter.

"The usual, Mr. Nickerson?" The man behind the counter asked.

"Thanks, Manny. This is my granddaughter, Debby, and her friend, Barbara," he said pointing to both of us as we slid onto the chrome-based stools, taking napkins from the metal container on the counter.

"I'm making doughnuts right now. How about some orange juice?"

We said "Yes" to both the doughnuts and the orange juice. Mr. Nickerson sat on a stool next to Debby and reached for the sugar container. He had a mug of coffee mixed with cream waiting in front of him on the counter. I watched as he measured two teaspoons of sugar and stirred them into his coffee. In a minute or so, we had fresh doughnuts, sitting on a dish before each of us.

"How's that?" Manny asked.

"Delicious," I said.

"Yummy," Debby replied.

After another round of doughnuts, we were back in Mr. Nickerson's black Pontiac, heading toward his home at 65 Nearwater Lane. Driving through stone and brick pillars at the beginning of the circular driveway, I noticed a large bronze statue of a dog on the lawn. Its raised head rose about four feet high as it stood at attention.

"That's a copy of our family dog, Duke. He died a few years ago," Mr. Nickerson said. "He was a great hunting dog, a pointer. I miss him, even today.

He parked the car near the entrance to his three-story, red-brick mansion, its windows trimmed in white with contrasting stone blocks of beige and gray, arching over the windows and doors. Slate shingles covered the roof and shielded the bay window out front. A filigree dominated the arched top and Corinthian columns flanked the front door. I had often admired the building when riding my bike to the beach but I had never been inside. I stepped into the wide entry, trailing Mr. Nickerson.

"Let me show you Grandpa's house," Debby said. Next to the banister leading to the upper floors, she moved from the foyer straight down the hallway toward the dining room. In the shadows under the staircase, a life-size suit of armor stared back at me. The metal plates would have covered a medieval man from the top of his head to the tips of his toes. Its silver metal helmet with numerous vertical visor slots seemed to hide evil eyes, eyes intent on harm and cruelty. I instantly felt anxious and decided to stay as far away from this figure as possible.

"The house was built sometime in the 1860s," Mr. Nickerson called as we walked past the suit of armor. "And the tent came from Morocco."

In the dining room, the walls and ceiling were covered with an authentic tent, as Mr. Nickerson had said, "from Morocco." Red and gold twisted braids hung strategically around the tent and a large table with twelve chairs filled the interior. A brass chandelier hung from the center; its dangling crystal pendants sparkled with gleams of light.

"Here's one sitting room," Debby said as we strolled into a room on the left. "We use it as our living room." Numerous vertical windows overlooked the flower garden in the backyard. Two sofas, a television, several tables, and numerous chairs decorated the room along with a large credenza filled with books, their colorful leather spines facing outward.

"And here's another sitting room," she said when we walked toward the front of the house. Between the two sitting rooms were enormous paneled doors that slid into side walls. When they were open, it became one gigantic room. I imagined elegant parties in front of the fireplace, drinking and dancing guests in formal attire. Mr. Nickerson had decorated the room from items he had purchased on his many international trips. The most striking items were the glass stems inside a blue vase. Not flowers, just stems. The Italian arrangement had been placed on top of a round table, draped with a fringed white cloth. Clear wisps of glass, thin strands that changed colors as they swayed with the slightest of breezes.

Across the foyer was another sitting room, probably the music room. The Nickerson family had a grand piano and a Victrola turntable made of mahogany and inlaid with speakers hidden behind black netting. A bar in the back corner held bottles of liquor, decanters, and glasses in all shapes and sizes. All the rooms had braided cords, hanging from the crown molding, a tassel attached to its end.

"What's this?" I asked, pointing at the cord.

"It's a bell cord," Debby answered. "You pull the cord when you want a servant to come into the room. Let me show you how it works."

She led me through the kitchen and pointed to a wooden plank near the ceiling. It had little bells with numbers underneath.

"When a cord is pulled, a bell rings," she explained. "The servant knows which number goes to which room. There's another box just like this in the basement."

I've always been afraid of the dark but with bright lights illuminating each room, I felt comfortable with my first, and only, encounter with the cement-floored basement. Below the house were rooms for coal storage and its furnace, washing tubs and drying lines, and vegetable and fruit bins.

Once Debby finished the basement tour, we climbed the stairs to the second and third floors. There were numerous bedrooms and two bathrooms, one on each level. She showed me a sleeping porch, a screened room to sleep in when summer temperatures became too hot to be inside. The Nickerson house was truly a grand mansion. It had all the comforts, for those not only in the 1860s but also for those in the 1950s.

A maid called us for lunch and we met with Mr. Nickerson at a table on the back patio. Debby's parents were away. I didn't ask about Mrs. Nickerson, not wanting to pry. It was only the three of us, eating sandwiches with lemonade, looking at the gardens and into the nearby woods and fields. He owned all the land from his house to Holly Pond.

After lunch, Mr. Nickerson left for his bedroom and the maid cleared the table and went into the kitchen. We picked out books to read and sat in the living room. After the obligatory half hour had ended, I suggested a game of hide and seek.

"I'll count to one hundred and then I'll try to find you. We'll stay on this floor only," I said. "No basement and no upstairs."

I stood and faced the bookshelf, my hands covering my eyes. Debby instantly left for parts unknown but I heard her feet scuffling along the hardwood floors.

"One, two, three, four," I counted until I reached one hundred. Turning around, I found no movement, no sound. *Where could she have gone?* I silently stepped into the front sitting room and looked under draped tables, behind upholstered chairs, and opened large cabinet doors. Nothing. From there I moved to the music room and stood in the center of the room and listened. A minute passed and then I heard movement behind one of the velvet curtains, hanging beside the front windows. I strode to the sound and pulled back the heavy drape. There she was.

"Debby! Good going. If I hadn't stood still for so long, I would never have found you," I said.

"That was fun. Now you hide," she said. Debby walked back to the living room and stood as I did, with her face toward the bookcase, her hands covering her eyes. As she counted, I went to the front sitting room and crept under the table with the sparkling Italian glass, its white linen cloth completely covering me. Kneeling with my head down, I stayed as quiet as possible.

"Where's Barbara?" I heard Mr. Nickerson ask as he entered the living room.

"We're playing hide and seek," Debby answered. "She's somewhere on this floor. I'm trying to find her."

"Okay. But don't break anything," he said. "You know how precious these things are to me. Especially the Venetian glass on the front table."

When I heard his words, I didn't dare move. No way would I want Mr. Nickerson to know that I was hiding underneath one of his most valuable possessions. I heard him walk into the kitchen and slowly crawled from underneath the linen-draped table.

"Here I am," I called to Debby.

"Oh, you didn't let me find you."

"I was afraid we might break something. Let's go upstairs and see what we can do there."

At the top of the stairs, Debby raised her leg and climbed onto the thick walnut banister. She sat, positioning herself in the middle, grabbing the upright column.

"Watch me."

She pushed off and slid down the handrail to the bottom. As soon as she collided with the newel post, bells rang throughout the three-story foyer, announcing her presence at the foot of the stairs. A string of sleigh bells had been wrapped around the column, its silver bells and red ribbons decorated the wooden pillar.

After a few more slides we gathered outside for another game of hide and seek. Then it was time for me to leave. Mr. Nickerson picked me up the following afternoon. Debby and I played hide and seek for the next few hours but only outside. No way did I want to tempt fate and break something. The house was definitely a mansion, but a warm and welcoming one, except for the suit of armor.

# OX RIDGE HUNT CLUB

Black flakes swirled in the autumn air. We looked out our school windows and watched dark objects floating from trees, from high above in the sky. Ash looking like snow. Soon sirens sounded, wailing through Darien, screaming one after the other. It was noon on Friday, 1957.

*What was going on?*

Someone whispered, "Ox Ridge. Ox Ridge's on fire."

*What? Is that true? What about the horses?*

After our school lunches we raced outside. John had removed his new transistor radio from his locker and turned it on, full blast for us to hear. We encircled him and understood that all three fire departments had been dispatched to the scene: Darien, Noroton, and Noroton Heights. Nine fire engines surrounded the famous hunt club, now engulfed in flames. Hay dust continued to explode, only adding to the confusion. Flames flew from one loft to another, consuming all three stable barns.

Grooms led frightened horses, kicking and rearing, from the thirty-year-old structures. Fearing for their lives, the horses attempted to return to their safe spots, their stalls. It took all the strength of the grooms and a few helpful spectators to keep them away from the fire. Seventy horses, many of them valuable show horses, were safely removed, all within half an hour. Despite blistering heat, thick smoke, and soaring flames. While ceilings buckled and hay bales crashed from the lofts above.

"I was at one of their horse shows just a few weeks ago," I said as we walked back to the classroom. "Cherry Lawn challenged Ox Ridge."

I recalled Sally and Ginny competing with me, riding around the indoor ring. We all won ribbons. I rode Chico, a beautiful piebald horse. White with huge black markings. Very large yet exceptionally gentle.

Watching television that night, I saw smoke and sparks, steam rising and drifting through the trees, up into the sky. Once the horses were safe, the firefighters broke bales of hay, scattering and soaking them over and over with water. They sprayed nearby buildings, drenching them, stopping any spread of flames.

Firemen emerged from the smoldering remains, soot and ash covering their uniforms and faces. We learned that many stayed the night to ward off any future fires, forestalling the threat of a second ignition. The local Salvation Army provided soup and each fire department's auxiliary units had coffee readily available. This allowed the firemen to keep working and sustain their energy.

Vans from nearby stables and neighboring towns assisted in relocating the displaced horses, some from as far away as Mt. Kisco, New York. Fifteen horses remained on the premises, to be used in riding instructions that would resume at the club. In spite of the fire, Ox Ridge Board of Stewards continued with its scheduled events: a Saturday dinner dance, a Sunday horseshow, and daily riding lessons. The riding ring and other buildings had been saved. In the entire complex, only the three stable barns had been destroyed.

It was revealed that a new ten-ton load of hay had just been delivered that morning. Speculation arose that the hay had been cut while not completely dry, possibly causing spontaneous combustion. No determination had been made at the time of the television broadcast.

# SENIOR HIGH
## 1958 – 1961

# CHANGING BODIES

Everywhere I looked in the high school halls, bodies were changing. Boys became taller, man-size and awkward. Muscles protruded from their shirts and their voices became lower and deeper. They grew wild in their urgency to prove themselves. Sucking hickies on a girlfriend's neck. Some bragged about getting to third base or even making a home run.

My girlfriends began to fill out, to become shapelier. Everyone but me. My chest was as flat as a board. Even with Kleenex filling my triple-A, padded bra, I felt homely and plain. In Home Economics class, the teacher mentioned wheat germ.

"Russian women eat a lot of wheat germ. And, guess what? They have large bosoms."

As soon as I returned home, I asked Mom to buy some wheat germ. In the next few months, I sprinkled granules of wheat on everything: cereal, sandwiches, steak, vegetables, even drinks. Nothing touched my lips until it had been dusted with wheat germ. I was obsessed. Determined to have some curves protruding from my chest, some ample breasts.

But nothing happened. I continued to stuff my bra with Kleenex, or even socks when I wore a bathing suit. Other girls were so large, they dug holes in the sand to place their breasts when lying face down on their beach towels. I didn't have to worry.

At night I curled my hair in rollers, blue with self-gripping spikes. Trying to make myself more attractive, more appealing, more desirable. After each shower, I rolled my wet strands and sat under a balloon-like, plastic bubble, its warm air blowing my hair dry. After twenty minutes or so, I finished with a simple style, either a pageboy or a flip. Or I just pulled my hair into a ponytail. I never had enough hair to twist into a beehive or bouffant. Two popular styles at high school that year.

Some of the boys began to reveal sideburns, long and thick in front of their ears. Some even showed tiny traces of mustaches above their lips. A few boys combed their hair in a "DA" style, shaping the backs of their hair to look like a Duck's Ass. Or they attempted the "waterfall," a curl falling from the middle of their foreheads, almost to their eyebrows. Elaborate hairstyles for both boys and girls became fashionable, the more extravagant the better. But not for everyone. Some boys had buzzcuts, crewcuts, or flattops, as simple as could be. And all the boys had rolled-up jeans or tan slacks with white socks in Weejun penny loafers or sneakers. Typical of teenagers, we all wanted to be accepted by our peers.

––––––––––––––

A few students were hired as grocery clerks on Friday nights, stacking cans of vegetables, and delivering groceries on Saturday mornings. On Monday, rumors were rampant.

"I saw a cop car parked outside one of my delivery houses," a classmate said. "Saw it numerous mornings.

Watched the cop tuck in his shirt and adjust his trousers as he left the house."

"Whose house?" I asked. "Which cop?"

"Not saying. I just think it's strange."

It wasn't easy but I tried to ignore the gossip, not to be swayed by the rumors. As Mom continuously reminded me, "If you can't say something nice, don't say anything at all."

# DARIEN HISTORY

"One of the roads in Darien is named 'Middlesex.' Do you know why?"

Mr. Harper taught U.S. history and specifically enlightened us about our town's rich past. The girls in the class didn't care what he instructed; he was so handsome. We sat at our desks, resting our chins on our palms, and stared at him. After his question, there was dead silence, and then some snickering came from the back of the room. A boy raised his hand.

"It means the street welcomes both women and men."

"No. It has nothing to do with sex. In this case, 'sex' is short for 'Saxon,'" he said. "You know, Anglo-Saxon."

"What'd you mean?" someone asked.

"The east section of Darien was once part of Norwalk, the west section was part of Stamford. In 1737, it broke free and was named, "Middlesex" because it was between the two main towns of Stamford and Norwalk. In the middle of them. The "sex" part of the word was the British spelling of Saxon. It came from England's counties of Sussex and Essex.

"Almost fifty years later, Moses Mather was hired as the first minister of Middlesex Parish. That was in 1820 at what is now the First Congregational Church. That's when Darien was officially incorporated."

Mr. Harper continued with Darien's history and how the town had been heavily involved in the Revolutionary War. He told how local British-sympathizing Tories disrupted church services and captured Reverend Mather along with a large group of worshiping men, transporting them across the Sound to Long Island.

"For five months, they suffered in British prisons in New York City with little food and in terrible conditions. Finally, they were released and returned to Darien."

By the time we left for recess, Darien's history had vanished. Nothing was on our minds but the latest singles. The sounds we heard from our radios or watched on *American Bandstand*. Elvis Presley's "Hound Dog," Buddy Holly's "That'll Be the Day," Jerry Lee Lewis' "Great Balls of Fire." For us, this new music was a soundtrack for rebellion. Music that sounded more exotic, more illicit than anything we had ever known. It was exciting, even stimulating, but not for our parents. "Turn that music down!"

# TAXI RIDE

"Want to join me for lunch tomorrow?" Dad asked. It was spring break and I had nothing special to do.

"Sure. Sounds like fun. Where do you want to meet?"

"Come to my office and we'll walk to a new restaurant. After lunch, you can shop. Join me on the 5:30 back to Darien."

Mom dropped me off at the Noroton Heights station at ten the next morning. I walked inside the weather-stained building and bought a roundtrip ticket at the office window. I had turned sixteen that autumn and this was my first time traveling to New York by myself. I didn't want to be late. A few women waited beside the New Haven railroad tracks, leaning forward to see if the black engine was coming into view. We all had on dresses; some included mink wraps, splashes of diamonds on their fingers and ears. I donned a London Fog trench coat over my wrap-around dress and sported a silver charm bracelet. As we were going into the "city," we all wore hats and gloves. Far up the track, we heard a loud whistle. The train approached, blowing steam into the air.

I sat in a nonsmoking car and stared out the window, losing myself, watching the passing woods and fields. A line of maple, elm, and ash trees whisked by, their leaves casting a light green tint, budding as they warmed.

"Ticket?" the conductor asked. He stood in a navy uniform with a navy cap on his head. I looked up and handed him my ticket. He punched it and placed it in a slot in the seatback in front of me.

About forty-five minutes later, brick tenements came into view. Clothes hung out windows and children played in the street. Huge painted billboards on the sides of the buildings advertised cigarettes and liquor. The train rumbled into the terminal and screeched to a stop. We had arrived in the cavernous darkness of the Manhattan station. I grabbed my purse and hat and adjusted my gloves. In the passageway, I gripped the railing and took the hand of the conductor standing below. With his guidance, I descended three steps to the cement platform.

"Thanks for the help," I said. He nodded to me and turned to ease the next passenger stepping from the train.

After climbing a wide staircase from the lower level and passing several newspaper stands, I strolled through the "whispering gallery." A place where you can hear the softest sounds over the din of crowds with your ear pressed against the Guastavino tiles, an acoustic oddity caused by the unusually perfect, self-supporting arches.

From there, I found my way into the enormous building, the iconic Grand Central Terminal, built by Cornelius Vanderbilt. Besides the three monstrous vertical windows, arched and imposing, I noticed a faded fresco of stars, zodiac symbols drawn on the teal-colored ceiling. As I stood, amazed by the main concourse, the sun sent a sheaf of golden rays onto the four-sided, Tiffany brass clock perched above the information booth. It had graced the top from the time the terminal had opened in 1913. Since I spent so much time with Uncle Jim, our next-door neighbor, I've always loved clocks. This one was particularly beautiful, especially since the metal workings were made by one of my favorite Connecticut clockmakers: Seth Thomas.

Because I wasn't sure how to walk to Dad's office, I decided to take a taxi. Wandering through the shadows of the enormous terminal, I found a sign that pointed to an outside door indicating a taxi stand. As I meandered to the door, I noticed a penny on Grand Central's marble floor. Bending over, I snatched the coin. This would be my lucky day.

"Forty-Seventh and Fifth," I said to the driver after I climbed into the yellow cab's backseat.

He drove up Madison Avenue and turned left on Forty-Eighth Street, merging into traffic and heading toward Fifth Avenue. I watched the meter rotate during the short trip. When he pulled in front of my stated address, he reached out to the meter's white flag and pushed it down. The gauge indicated seventy-five cents. Knowing I should tip ten percent, I stood outside the cab and handed the driver three quarters and a dime. More than ten percent. I knew he'd be happy.

"Thank you very much," I said, smiling as I leaned in the window.

"You need this more than me," he shouted and threw the dime into my face. It missed me and rolled onto the sidewalk. I was absolutely shocked by his reaction. I turned away as the cab skidded from the curb. With tears brimming in my eyes, I heard the screech of wheels and saw spitting gravel flying around me. I knelt and retrieved the dime.

*"What did I do? What about the lucky penny?"*

His angry reaction filled my thoughts as I walked toward the entrance of the Longines-Wittnauer Building. My father managed the thirty-four-story property and the one next to it. The second building faced Forty-Seventh Street, flanking the largest diamond district in the world.

As I passed under one of the building's gigantic Fifth Avenue arches, a gentleman held the door open for me. Streams of people were leaving. I mingled between them, past a newsstand, toward the elevators.

"Going up. Face the front, please," an elevator operator said in a deep voice as I stepped into the compartment. Dressed in a brown uniform, he shut the door and slid the metal grid across the front.

"What floor, please?"

Everyone in the elevator turned to face the front and gave him a floor number. He punched in the numbers on a brass plate and tilted a lever to begin the ascent. We watched the floors pass on the other side of the charcoal-colored grid, all of us standing quietly together. When we reached the fourth floor, the elevator stopped. The operator slid the grid open and then reached out and pushed open the door.

I stepped into a light blue hallway and walked to my father's door. When I entered his outer office, Mrs. Furlong, an older woman with her hair tied in a bun, was bending intently over her typewriter. She looked up and greeted me with a smile.

"Hi, Barbara. Your dad's in a meeting. It's just about over. They'll be out any moment."

As she finished her sentence, Dad's office door opened. A man walked out of the oak-paneled room, tilted his hat at me, and exited the reception area. My father strolled toward me, dressed in a dark suit with a blue boutonniere in his lapel.

"Where're you going for lunch?" Mrs. Furlong asked.

"I have reservations at the Top of the Sixes," Dad answered as he brushed tiny pieces of lint from the sleeve of his jacket. "It just opened a few weeks ago."

"I want to hear all about it," Mrs. Furlong said.

Dad put on a black fedora hat, looked in a mirror, tilting the brim. We left his office, heading toward the elevator. Once outside, we dodged our way through the crowded sidewalk, past Rockefeller Center to 666 Fifth Avenue. I kept my eyes focused straight ahead, on the backs of people's heads. I didn't want to tell Dad about the taxi driver. Not yet.

A uniformed man held the building's door for us and we passed into gold-trimmed elevators, getting off on the forty-first floor. Dad led me to the maître d', a man in a dark suit standing behind a wooden podium, and gave his name.

"Right this way, Mr. Phelps," he said.

I followed him to a window table as customers turned to inspect the new arrivals. He pulled out a chair for me and Dad walked around and sat with his back to the city view. It was spectacular.

"May I take your drink orders?" a waitress asked. Dressed in a black skirt and white blouse with a red cinch belt, she looked beautiful.

"I'll have a martini," Dad said. "What do you want?" he said as he looked across the table at me.

"I'll have iced tea."

After she left, I told Dad what happened on my taxi ride to his office. He became angry and gave way to his prejudices.

"Well, he probably wanted you to give him a dollar but that was no way to act. He wouldn't have done that if I had been in the cab."

Then a tirade of ethnic slurs emerged. He was furious. Whenever we talked at home about dating, he always said he wanted us to date a white, Anglo-Saxon, Protestant. In other words, a "WASP." He was insistent that Ginny and I follow his advice.

Next, we gave our lunch orders after looking through the thin, black menus. Dad switched to iced tea with lemon. While we ate, I told him about a babysitting job, being a nanny for a New Canaan family that had a summer place in Old Lyme, Connecticut.

"They want me for the whole summer. For their two boys."

"Is that what you want to do?" The familiar smell of his cigarette clouded the air as he leaned back, questioning my option.

"The money's good but the stepdad doesn't want the boys near him. He's not very nice. The mom's wonderful but she wants me to keep her sons busy. They're five and seven. What do you think?"

"It doesn't sound like you want to do that. When Mrs. Furlong goes on vacation, why not work for me?"

"Are you serious? That would be fabulous. I'd love to do that!"

We talked about the work I could do at his office and how much I could learn. Then Dad told me about special tickets he had obtained for Ginny and me. Tickets to see Elvis and Jerry Lee Lewis. That copper penny I found turned out to be lucky after all.

# THE DIAMOND DISTRICT

One of the front windows at the Longines-Wittnauer building displayed Olivetti typewriters. Around the corner on Forty-seventh Street was the heart of the Diamond District. It comprised only one block, between Fifth and Sixth Avenues (the Avenue of the Americas). Hasidic Jews with their black frock coats, black hats, and long curling sideburns, occupied the nearby offices. Cutting, polishing, grading, trading, and selling diamonds.

Taking a lunch break from being a receptionist at Dad's business for the past two weeks, I asked if he would take me to a diamond company on one of the upper floors.

"Okay. Let's go," Dad said.

We exited the elevator on the eighth floor and walked down the narrow hallway to Room 806 and entered a small enclosed room, maybe four-by-six feet. As soon as we stepped into the cubicle, the door behind us locked. Dad tapped on a one-way mirror in front of us. A person behind the window could see us but we couldn't see him. After he realized it was my father, he unlocked a second door. We heard a click and the door to our right opened. The jewelry company had created a safety barrier, locking us inside the cubicle until they recognized us.

We were directed to a separate workplace and sat on chairs facing a man my father knew. Dad introduced me to Mr. Kaufman who stood behind the desk. His head looked like a boulder under his hat with dark curls flowing from each side, above his ears and tumbling down his cheeks. He spilled diamonds from white tissue paper buried in his frock pocket onto the top of the desk. He unwrapped the diamonds one at a time and withdrew a loupe from his breast pocket. Adjusting his jeweler's lamp, he tilted the shade so it shined directly on each diamond. With the loupe to his eye, he bent over and examined the diamonds.

"Look at this one, Barbara," he said. "It's the best one I have. Only a few flaws."

I took another loupe and put it to my eye, staring at the diamond, now placed on a black velvet cloth.

"Wow. It's beautiful."

"Maybe someday, you'll be wearing a diamond like that," Dad said, standing behind me beaming. "You'll need a serious boyfriend first."

"Oh, Dad. You know I'm too young. Maybe after college."

"You're right. After college," he said. "A girl only needs two years of college so it won't be long. Four years from now and you'll be ready."

As we stood to leave, I extended my hand. I wanted to show the man how professional I was. He quickly put his hands behind his back and nodded at my father.

"Okay. Let's go," Dad said as he put his palms on my shoulders and turned me toward the exit. "Thanks, Mr. Kaufman. I appreciate your time."

Once again, we were in the cubicle, waiting for the door to be bolted behind us before the door to the hallway was unlocked. It was the jeweler's form of security. One that was used throughout the Diamond District.

Out in the corridor, I asked, "Why didn't he shake my hand?"

"They're not allowed to touch women who aren't members of their family. It's part of their religion," Dad said. "They even ride separate buses when commuting from Brooklyn. Amazingly, most deals are made with a handshake and a Yiddish blessing. But only with men. Here, your word is your bond. It's paramount in the diamond district."

# MICHAEL WEED

After years of babysitting and lawn mowing, I had saved a few hundred dollars, mostly in ones and fives, stuffed into a jar on my bedroom dresser. I had taped a picture of a horse to the outside of the glass container and Dad had punctured a slit on its lid. My family knew of my hoarding, saving money for a horse.

"Look at this," Mom said one Saturday morning. She showed me a classified advertisement in the *Darien Review*. A palomino mare was for sale in New Canaan and the asking price was two hundred dollars.

Excited and taking the newspaper from Mom, I rushed to the phone in the downstairs hallway and called the number. The woman on the phone, Mrs. Jones, said the price included the tack: bridle, saddle and pad, halter, and lead rope.

"She's five years old and gentle," Mrs. Jones said. "She's just a peach."

"Mom and I'll drive up to see her," I said. "Probably this afternoon. I have a lawn to cut in a few minutes. Is that okay?"

"Perfect. I'll be waiting."

An elderly couple owned the house across from ours on Outlook Drive. They were pleased to have me do their mowing and trimming each week. And I made a dollar for the effort. It was an easy job and they usually tipped me a quarter.

After mowing and changing my clothes to jodhpurs and knee-high boots, I joined Mom in the Chevy. On the way out the driveway, Mom asked me what I planned for a stable.

"I checked the Franklin's barn, but it was in poor shape," I said. "Plus, they don't want another horse in their enclosure. I'm still looking."

"Let's stop here," she said as we turned off the Post Road and began our way up Noroton Avenue. We both had noticed a sturdy barn behind the white house near the corner of the two main roads.

Once Mom paused in the driveway, I opened the car door, climbed out, and confidently strolled to the front door. After ringing the bell, Mrs. Miller, the associate minister's wife, appeared at the entrance. She had thick brown hair and wore a blue dress with a floral apron. I introduced myself and inquired about the barn.

"Come in," she said as she held the door open and stepped to the side.

Standing in the foyer, I told her about buying a horse and owning it for the three months of summer. "I'd sell it before school begins in the fall."

"As long as you keep everything neat and clean, we'd enjoy having a horse in the barn," she stated. "It's an old barn but very sturdy. There are three stalls, made for cows, but a horse will fit. We won't charge anything."

"I'll be back tomorrow to scrub and sweep," I said, a wide smile blanketing my face. "Thank you very much!"

I practically skipped to Mom's car, I was so happy.

"Well, what'd they say?"

"Mrs. Miller said 'okay' and at no charge. I just have to keep everything neat. I told her I'd be over tomorrow to clean."

When Mom and I arrived at our destination in New Canaan, we parked behind the house and walked toward a fenced-in shed. In the paddock stood a gorgeous golden palomino mare with a silver mane and tail. It was love at first sight. While leaning on a top rail, staring at the horse, a woman approached us.

"Her name is Blondie," she said. "She's beautiful, isn't she?"

"Yes, she is," I said. "My name is Bobbi and this is my mother, Florence Phelps." They shook hands and Mrs. Jones introduced herself.

"Want to ride her?"

"Yes, please."

Mrs. Jones entered the paddock and holding Blondie's halter, she led her to the shed. In a few minutes they both emerged. Blondie had on an English saddle and pad along with a snaffle bit and reins. The single mouthpiece fit easily in her mouth.

"I'll give you a leg up," she offered.

"Thanks," I said as I crawled between the railings. When I was next to Blondie, I bent my left knee and Mrs. Jones helped to lift me as I swung my right leg over the horse's back. While she held the reins, I adjusted the stirrups. Picking up the reins, I walked Blondie around the gravel paddock. With a slight kick of my heels, she trotted in a small loop beside the fence while I posted, rising up and down in the saddle to the beat of her body. With a tiny pull on the reins, she stopped and we walked in a continuing circle. I turned her head toward the fence, leaned over her opposite shoulder, and touched her side with my heels. She obediently began a slow, rocking canter. After two turns around the paddock, we stopped and I encouraged her to walk toward Mom and Mrs. Jones.

"Well, what do you think?" Mrs. Jones inquired.

"Oh, she's perfect," I answered, smiling from ear to ear. "I'd like to buy her."

"Barbara," Mom said, "you can't do that yet. We don't have any feed. And you haven't cleaned the barn."

"May I give you a deposit?" I asked Mrs. Jones.

We settled on my giving her fifty dollars that day and the remaining amount when I picked up Blondie the following week, after the last day of high school, before summer vacation.

On our way home, we stopped at a feed store and I ordered ten bales of hay, some straw, and a large bag of oats. Everything was arranged to be delivered to the Miller's barn. But not for five days.

After church the next day, I changed my clothes and drove to the white house behind the Presbyterian Church, the car's trunk stocked with cleaning supplies: broom, mop, bucket, rags, dustpan, and Pine Sol. The main floor of the barn had three bays, two for cars and a third for storage. The area underneath the bays once held three cows, each one in its own straight stall. There was also a wire-enclosed space for me to store the oats and tack. Another section near the front door was where I'd place the bales of straw and hay.

I began to scrub the walls, sweep and mop the cement floor, and wash the windows, practically obsessed with my project. Spiders encased their webs between rafters. Cobwebs filled the corners in the cow stalls. An older man, with a mustache and wearing a straw hat, came into the barn and introduced himself.

"Hi. I work for Mr. and Mrs. Miller. My name's Frank."

"Hi. I'm Bobbi," I said, wiping sweat from my brow as I leaned on the mop.

"I'll bring a pitchfork and shovel for you to use. When the horse arrives, just throw the manure out the back door," he said. "It'll be too hot to use in the garden. But after a week or so, the manure'll be perfect for the field."

"Thanks. I'll do that," I said. "She'll be arriving next Saturday. I have to ride her from New Canaan, so we probably won't be here until the late afternoon."

"Let me know if I can do anything to help."

"Thanks, Frank," I said as I bent to pick up the water bucket.

The following Saturday, clear and bright, turned out to be a wonderful day for riding. I cut the neighbor's yard and then changed into my riding clothes. Mom drove me to New Canaan, my remaining money still in its jar, sitting on my lap. Mrs. Jones had Blondie tied to the fence, saddled and ready when we arrived.

"That's going to be quite a ride you're doing today," she said.

"I've been riding since I was five, but I've never ridden long-distance. I think it's nine or ten miles," I said as I brought out my jar of money. While I counted out one hundred and fifty dollars, Mrs. Jones handed Mom a small cardboard box stuffed with horse items: a rubber curry comb, a wood-handled brush, a metal mane/tail comb, shampoo, and a hoof pick.

"Blondie is my last horse," Mrs. Jones said. "We're moving to Chicago. I'll still ride but I won't own any horses." I noticed her eyes brimming with tears. Embarrassed, I turned away to pull down the stirrups and mount Blondie. She quivered with excitement as I arranged the reins.

"Thanks for all the extras," I said after I was properly seated in the saddle. "That will save me quite a bit of money."

When I picked up the reins, Mrs. Jones opened the paddock gate. I was on my way to Noroton Avenue. I waved to Mrs. Jones and followed Mom's car out the driveway toward South Avenue. I watched the turquoise Chevy disappear from sight as I continued my ride. It was almost noon and the June heat was building. Houses along the road, their hedges highlighted with carnations and roses, daisies and lilies, enhanced the ride as scents hung thick in the morning air.

When we crossed the bridge over the Merritt Parkway, I was surprised Blondie did not seem bothered by the moving traffic below her. She easily walked over the concrete crossing. As soon as we touched the other side of the bridge, the road changed to Mansfield Avenue. I eased into the rhythm of Blondie's pace and we continued another mile or so. Mom waited for me at the corner of Middlesex Road. She trusted I knew the directions to the Miller's barn from there.

On the ride from New Canaan to Darien, I thought of a new name for my horse. I didn't like "Blondie." Even though she was a mare, I loved the name "Michael." And being a history buff, I knew the "Weed" family were early settlers in Darien. I named her Michael Weed.

Two miles after waving to Mom, I came upon a bridge that crossed the New York/New Haven railroad tracks, near the Noroton Heights Station. With more traffic and numerous overhead wires and black girders, Blondie began to prance, trotting sideways, dancing back and forth. Her muscles rippling with nervousness, she felt uneasy about the site. There was no way I could walk her on the narrow sidewalk with its low railing. I felt my resolve diminish, scattering through the air. *Could we make it over the bridge? What else could I do?* I had to continue. Shortening the reins, I stopped, twisting in the saddle to see a break in the vehicle traffic. Once it was clear, I trotted her over the bridge. On the opposite side, she calmed as I steered her over another bridge, across the newly finished Connecticut Turnpike. It had opened a few months earlier and there wasn't much traffic. I directed her to a wide sidewalk and plodded the last half mile, down the slope of Noroton Avenue.

Mom waited in her car, reading a book, when I rode toward the barn. I was exhausted. Although it had taken only a little over two hours, I had never ridden in traffic or crossed bridges on a horse. Plus, before starting the riding venture, I had mowed the neighbor's lawn.

"You've done a great job," Mom said as she joined me in the stable. "The place smells of Pine Sol and looks wonderful."

Struggling with a sore butt, legs, and arms, I could barely undo the girth belt and lift the saddle from Michael Weed's back, I trudged to the second stall and placed them on the half wall. I felt drained. Mom watched me take the halter and remove the bridle. I dipped the bit into a clean water bucket, wiped it dry, and hung the bridle on a protruding hook.

"Here," Mom said as she handed me a carrot. "Give her this." Mom had been a topnotch equestrian when she was young, winning numerous ribbons at horse shows in the South. She loved horses and was helpful throughout my process of acquiring the Palomino mare.

I held out the carrot and Michael Weed stretched her neck to take it. Her chin hairs tickled my fingers. I rubbed behind her ears and she made low humming noises, her lips quivering into what looked like a smile. Now that my mare was in the barn, standing in thick straw, she seemed absolutely content, purring like a cat.

From that day on, I rode Michael Weed every day – usually in the afternoon or early evening after swimming at the Noroton Bay Beach Club. Frank had offered to throw hay and fill the water bucket in the morning. I did the mucking, riding, and feeding in the afternoon.

A month later I regaled my high school friends with stories of riding to the Tastee-Freeze and around the field between the new and old Hindley schools, as well as along Nearwater Lane to my house on Outlook. Jenny asked if she could join me.

"Of course," I said. "Let's meet at two. I'll be riding in the Hindley Schoolyard." Jenny drove in her brand-new sportscar to the parking lot with Karen, another classmate. They waved to me and quickly emerged from her beige convertible.

"Can we ride?" they asked.

"Sure. I've been on her for about an hour. She'll be waiting for someone new," I said as I dismounted, brushing off my jeans and sneakers.

Holding the reins, I helped Jenny onto the saddle. I next bent Karen's knee so I could toss her behind Jenny. The two of them began to circle the playground, just walking and familiarizing themselves with Michael Weed's manner. When the mare began to trot, Karen began to bounce. Holding onto Jenny's waist, she inadvertently kicked the mare's flank. Again and again.

The unevenness of the two on her back obviously bothered my mare. Michael Weed turned her head and trotted toward a tree, advancing below a large, low-hanging limb. She ducked her head and continued trotting. Jenny's eyes went from sparkling to bright and wide as Michael Weed approached the tree. The heavy branch hit Jenny first and then swept both girls off her back. Karen fell first into the dirt and Jenny fell right on top of her. Without a backward glance, Michael Weed was off, galloping across the schoolyard, stirrups and reins flying into the air. She jumped the stone wall, crossed the Post Road, and raced up Noroton Avenue. Horns blew and trucks swerved, blowing black diesel smoke from their exhausts.

Horrified, I dashed after her. Flooded with emotions, I imagined terrible things. *Would a vehicle hit her? Would she fall and break a leg?* I threw up my arms and traffic stopped in all directions. Drivers watched as I ran, pounding the pavement as I followed her toward the Miller's barn.

Mr. and Mrs. Miller were hosting a garden party in their backyard as Michael Weed approached. Three tables blocked her way to the lower barn. Tiny sandwiches with their crusts removed, sliced fruit and vegetables, deviled eggs, and desserts covered the white cloths. In the middle of each table, a large punch bowl rested between the desserts and hors d'oeuvres.

All the ladies wore flowered dresses with straw bonnets and colorful ribbons. The men were attired in summer suits in several pastel shades. Their hair slicked back, glistening with pomade. The guests gasped and moved to the side as Michael Weed advanced at a fast pace toward them. Blocked by the tables, she halted at their edges. Seeing a large bowl, she plunged her face into the pink punch.

"Oh, no," I screamed. With tears streaming down my face, I grabbed her bridle and pulled her from the table as she slobbered punch over the snacks and table cloth. I was mortified.

"I'm so sorry," I whimpered.

"Oh, don't worry," Mrs. Miller said as she wrapped an arm around my shoulders. "This is the highlight of my garden party. No one will be able to beat this one."

What a sweetheart. I couldn't believe how nice she was to me after such a disastrous occasion. I walked Michael Weed around the opposite side of the barn and entered the back door. After removing her bridle and feeding her, I joined Jenny and Karen where they had parked on Noroton Avenue. I had the rest of the story they'd want to hear.

When the summer ended, I sold Michael Weed to the woman who ran the riding academy at Cherry Lawn School on Brookside. The majority of faculty members and students at the private institute were Jewish. A surprising statistic since the school was located in Darien, a restricted town. I had been riding at Cherry Lawn for ten years and the director was glad to have a horse of her own. She renamed her "Naomi."

# THE CONGREGATIONAL CHURCH

On Christmas Eve that year, Ginny and I arrived at the Congregational Church, just before eleven o'clock. It was a teenage tradition to participate in a midnight candle-lighting ceremony, whether you belonged to the church or not.

The initial Congregational Church was built in 1744 and had a tumultuous history. Moses Mather was the first minister who gained notoriety by being one of the first to preach against British rule. The church also protected runaway slaves and was part of the Underground Railroad.

When we entered, its unadorned design indicated a typical New England meetinghouse. Straightforward, simplistic, and fundamental. Ginny and I sat on hard benches in the balcony, looking at plain rows of dark wooden seats, highlighted against the white painted walls and pew boxes. The church didn't offer a sermon and no choir serenaded us. It was the congregation that sang Christmas carols that night. A few local dignitaries stood to read from the Bible, the Gospel According to Luke, Chapter 2.

*And it came to pass in those days, that there went out a decree from Caesar Augustus that all the world should be taxed.*

The selected notables came forward and read section after section, describing Joseph and Mary coming to Bethlehem and Jesus in the manger *because there was no room for them in the inn.*

The last carol was "Silent Night." Soft, sweet voices filled the nave. When the minister approached the altar, the congregation followed in orderly rows, carrying candles to be lit by the assistant minister. Ginny and I left the church with our flaming candles and gathered outside to talk with friends. I added my candle to the others in the snow and walked with Ginny back to our car.

I steadied her candle on my lap as we drove from the parking lot. Passing the white-steepled church, surrounded with candles burning in the snow, we marveled at the sight. The true meaning of Christmas had come to Darien.

By the time we arrived home, Ginny's candle had only a couple inches left of wax. We placed it in a metal holder on the piano and she played a few single notes, then chords, using both hands to find harmonies for us to sing. "The First Noel," "We Three Kings," "Joy to the World." Mom, Dad, and Gail joined in. Once the candle had taken its last breath, Ginny tweaked the wick, eliminating the flame, and we settled around the Christmas tree. Dad gave us our one present, always new pajamas or nighties, so we would look nice for photos the following morning.

When I woke on Christmas morning, I noticed my glass jar still filled with money, sitting on my bedroom dresser. I had been saving my babysitting money for two months. The jar had a newspaper clipping wrapped around it, advertising a beautiful model wearing a rabbit ski parka with a wolf fur collar and leather Eskimo trim.

It came from B. Altman's in New York City. The price of seventy dollars was too steep for my family to give as a Christmas gift. Mom said, "If you can earn half, Dad and I will kick in the rest." Saving every penny only garnered twenty-nine dollars, not quite enough.

After breakfast we started, one by one, opening presents. Following a morning filled with laughter and surprises, we knew our next task was to write thank-you letters. Before we could play with a gift or wear a new piece of clothing, we had to write a thank-you note. It was our mother's rule.

Before this ritual, we helped clean the living room. Creating a pile of boxes, neatly folding wrapping paper, and adding bows to a brown bag, all to be reused at birthdays and holidays. Passing through the foyer, Mom asked if I received everything I wanted.

"Of course."

I did receive some wonderful presents. There was no way I would be rude or hurt anyone's feelings. And I would never mention the ski parka I so desperately wanted. Dad and Mom stood next to each other, near the staircase, looking at me.

"Well, then. We'll just have to take back the package that's still in the closet," she said pointing toward the left side of the front door.

I turned and grabbed the handle, practically ripping it from its mount. There on the floor sat a brightly wrapped box. I looked at Mom and Dad. They each had huge smiles on their faces. Tearing into the package, I grasped the fur ski parka I had wanted and held it up. I couldn't believe it!

"But Mom, the jar's still full."

"That's all right. Dad and I saved extra this year. Merry Christmas."

I immediately donned the parka, pulling the hood over my head, the wolf fur circling my face. Dancing into the living room, I showed my sisters what I looked like in my latest gift.

"You look beautiful," Gail said.

"You'll look great on the slopes. Now if you could only ski," Ginny added with a teasing smile.

I pushed her in mock protest and twirled to show her the back of the parka.

"I love it! You're right, Gail. I feel beautiful."

# TILLEY POND

Arctic air hurled into Connecticut, plunging Darien into an unusually bitter winter that January. Driven by northern winds, temperatures dropped steadily until they reached below zero. During one specific afternoon, fresh and biting, Ginny drove Gail and me to Tilley Pond, a private park originally owned by George Dudley Tilley, the prolific buyer and seller of exotic water birds. His birds populated estates, conservancies, and zoos around the world. After he died in 1946, his widow allowed the local children to use the pond for skating. And skate we did.

After the pond froze to a thick crust and school was closed, boys arrived early to shovel mounds of snow from the ice. They needed smooth surfaces for their hockey games. Bits of hardened snow skittered across the ice as they pushed their broad-bladed shovels back and forth, over and over, across the frozen pond.

After we parked on West Avenue; Ginny, Gail, and I climbed the stone wall and trudged over three inches of crunchy snow. Ginny found Sally and Dottie, her high school friends, already sitting on nearby logs. Gail strode to another log, uniting with her own buddies. I joined Ginny, replacing my boots with my freshly polished, white ice skates. I laced my skates, took a deep breath, and using rubber guards over the blades, wobbled to the water's edge. Before stepping onto the ice, I noticed a line of bare trees surrounding the pond, icicles hanging from their branches and sparkling in the late day's sun. Magical. Thick ribbons of smoke from house fireplaces meandered through the air. A beautiful day for skating but bitter and cold.

Ginny skated with her girlfriends while I skimmed over the ice, looking for classmates. Holly, her warm hazel eyes peering out from under the rim of her wool hat, dashed toward me. Strands of curly brown hair emerged, circling her friendly face. Medium in height and build but exceptionally athletic from years of competitive swimming, she skated with abandon.

"It's about time," she said. "We've been waiting for you so we could do some figure eights. Are you going to join us?"

"Of course," I said as I followed her to the near end of the pond.

Dawn, Linda, Sarah, and Sherry started the procession. Holly and I followed as we skated in large, lazy circles. After a few "eights," we watched Sherry slide neatly on the smooth surface before pirouetting and stopping with one skate pierced into the ice. She had the form and grace of a professional.

"Are we ever impressed," Linda called. "That was super!"

Our knot of girls gathered to skate a series of figure eights in a backward motion, moving our hips back and forth as we completed the circles. Clear droplets of ice beaded on the fuzz of my wool jacket and I brushed them off, my breath smoking. After two hours of skating in the freezing air, I gave up.

"It's too cold," I complained. "I'm getting my sisters."

Silver threads of snow tapped my shoulders as I skated toward Ginny. Gail was already on a log, having removed her skates and sat with her friends, scrutinizing the pick-up game of hockey, its players racing up and down the far end of the pond. I recognized Dave, Alan, Jack, and John. As goalie, Ken stood before the pretend net, a semi-circle of rocks. He bent forward, ready to pounce, to block the black puck. His feet spaced wide apart with his knees together, almost touching each other.

We heard the clashing of sticks, clapping of skates, and noisy yells from the guys as they tore over the pond. They glided back and forth, turning and circling, thrusting the puck over the ice. We watched them skate past the far end of Tilley's stone hut, their breaths streaming into the cold air. Only the silver etchings on the ice from their skates indicated that they had once been close to our side of the pond.

Gail smacked her mittened hands against each other and stamped her feet, trying to encourage circulation into her extremities. She blew into her cupped hands and hugged her body, trying to warm up. The sky turned slowly to thick white flakes, looking as dazzling as diamonds in the late afternoon, the sun's rays cutting through the gathering clouds.

"Time to go," I yelled to Ginny. She must have read my mind. She was already skating toward us when I called. After we exchanged our skates for boots, we traipsed to the car, our skate laces tied to each other and slung over our shoulders. One skate in front, the other in back.

"I think it's time for hot chocolate," Ginny said. "Race you to the car!"

With the challenge still ringing in our ears, we pivoted in the wind of the collecting storm and were off. All three girls running toward the Chevy, our white skates bouncing from our shoulders.

# YOUNG LIFE

We bowed our heads and waited for devotions, sitting at wooden tables flanked by long, oak benches. This was the beginning of my two enjoyable weeks in the Adirondacks at a Young Life camp. Swimming, waterskiing, canoeing, and Christian fellowship.

During the previous school year, I had met with numerous friends every Tuesday night in a living room of a private home for two hours of singing and worship. Jack, Dean, and Coe, graduates from Wheaton College in Illinois, led the weekly activities in Darien and now at the summer camp in Upstate New York.

"We give thanks for the food, thanks for another beautiful day, and thanks to those who came to know Christ as their Savior."

We reflected on what Jack had prayed and after a pause, he said, "Let's eat."

Toward the end of the first week at camp, I wandered off by myself and took a seat on a boulder overlooking the camp's lake and considered Jack's prayer. The warm evening surrounded me with tranquility. A soft breeze rustled the leaves overhead. I felt at peace as I sat with a Bible in my lap and turned to John 3:16.

*For God so loved the world, that He gave His only begotten Son, that whosoever believeth in Him should not perish, but have everlasting life.*

God had invited me to accept His Son, to believe in Him. I bowed my head and asked Christ to come into my life and to lead me. There on a large, rugged stone, beside a lake in the Adirondacks, I accepted the Lord.

Walking from the lake along a path back to the lodge, I felt in total harmony. With a smile on my face, I entered my cabin and joined three other girls sitting on their bunk beds.

"Something good happened to you?" one of them asked.

"Yes, I accepted the Lord."

"So did we. Isn't that wonderful? Let's give Him thanks."

We sat together and prayed aloud, my first time saying a prayer for others to hear. After climbing under our covers, listening to the old bunk beds groan from the weight of our bodies, we talked about our activities planned for the next few days. Mumbling about who would waterski, who would waitress, who would help run the camp games?

During the beginning of the following week, a dilapidated secondhand school bus arrived from New York City, dark gray smoke billowing from its tailpipes. Tough, rowdy teens from the Lower East Side filled the interior. Before boarding back in New York, they had to give up their knives. They knew not to carry guns.

Jenny and I met Joey and Enzo in the lodge's game room. With greased hair formed into a "DA" and white tank tops exposing their muscles, they demonstrated the game of pool. Were they ever good! Totally breaking the initial pyramid of balls, using cue sticks to bounce balls off the felt rail into leather pockets, and calling and making shots.

During their week at camp, the New York teens turned their lives around. They impressed everyone with their perseverance and energy. Having had little or no water experiences, they tried swimming and some of them attempted water skiing. Most of them accepted the Lord.

Before they returned to the City, Jenny and I told Joey and Enzo that we'd meet at their church three hours before a Young Life meeting, a few weeks in the future. As the dilapidated bus chugged from the campgrounds, they waved out the windows, wide smiles on their faces.

Once the date arrived, Jenny and I rode a train into Manhattan. From there, we took a taxi to the boys' church, a stone and brick edifice with steps leading to a basement. Joey and Enzo stood outside the building, waiting for us. Our parents knew we were attending a Young Life meeting in the city. They didn't know we were meeting without any chaperone in the Lower East Side, a section of working poor, living in almost slum conditions. A known crime-ridden area of Manhattan.

When the four of us departed the church, I noticed Italian elders sitting on front steps, eating and smoking, gesturing with their hands. Beer bottles and trash littered the streets. Stray cats roamed the alleys.

In a few blocks, Joey and I turned in the opposite direction of the other two and entered his tenement building, climbing to the second floor, arriving at his apartment. His parents sat around a small table in the kitchen, drinking coffee and chatting.

"Hi. Glad you came."

His mother stood and offered me coffee, stepping to the stove and turning on the gas, heating a metal pot.

"No, thank you. I'm fine. May I have some water?"

She brought a glass to the table, putting a napkin beside it. Joey and I sat on the two vacant chairs.

"Where you goin'?" his father asked.

"I'll show her around. Then to church."

I noticed another door, slightly ajar, leading to the bedroom. That was it. A two-room apartment with a communal bathroom down the building's hall. I had no idea where Joey slept. I didn't ask.

When we strolled through other parts of his neighborhood, I spotted a heavy woman watering pots of geraniums, all in different shades of red. Next to her curled a cat, sleeping in the sunlight. Nearby an old man walked a brown mutt, a tiny dog who lifted his leg on a small bush. Children played catch on the sidewalk across the street. Another man sat on a bench and read a newspaper, lowering it to gaze at us. Pigeons bobbed at his feet, picking at something on the ground, waiting for a possible crumb to drop. All seemed relatively peaceful. Not at all like the image my parents had of the Lower East Side.

As we walked, Joey told me more about himself. I knew he was a captain but I wasn't sure of what. I found out he belonged to some sort of gang. He demanded all able-bodied boys in his neighborhood to join the gang. Vandalism, bullying, and thefts were their motivation.

Along the way we met one of Joey's friends, a teen with an unusual and awkward limp.

"Hey, Joey. What's up?"

"Hey, Angelo. This is Bobbi. Where you going?"

"To the store. Mom wants some coffee."

"Why's he limping?" I asked after he had left. "Did he have an accident?"

"No. He wanted to leave the gang," Joey answered. "He didn't want any more to do with gangs. So, I shot him in the knee."

I stared in disbelief. "I thought he was your friend."

"Better than killing him."

We continued our walk, my mind reeling from Joey's comment. What a different world he lived in. Still in a gang and trying to live a life with Christ. Eventually, we joined Jenny and Enzo along with other teens at the Young Life meeting, downstairs in the cement-floored basement. We sat on folding chairs and listened to Dean and Jack talk about Christ and how they wanted us to lead the "Good Life." We stood when Coe led us in song, praising the Lord. In spite of the attendance of maybe thirty youths, I felt there would be few who could keep their promises to God in such a harsh environment. In such a tough neighborhood. I found out three months later that Joey had gone back to his gang ways. Even worse. Now, he was heavily involved in drugs.

# BURNING RUBBER

I tied a short, red scarf around my ponytail and fastened a gold circle pin on the left side of my blouse. Wearing nylons, a colorful scarab bracelet, and black flats; I dressed similarly to the other girls in our high school. I bought from the same stores, wore the same styles, and never wanted to look differently. Once I was ready and by the French doors fronting our back porch, Elsa arrived. She pulled into our driveway, steering her Mom's station wagon.

"Elsa's here, Mom. We'll be back in a few hours."

Elsa maneuvered the car up Nearwater Lane, to the Post Road. St. Luke's Episcopal Church, its tall steeple rising to a gold cross on top, sat on the corner to Rings End Road. I glanced at the spire, seeing it embraced by the sun, the cross glistening as Elsa turned right, taking the sloping road to its very end.

We talked about the loss of our favorite singers a few months earlier. Buddy Holly, Ritchie Valens, and the Big Bopper had died in a plane crash. During a heavy, February snowstorm. Now it was spring and we were looking forward to meeting friends, watching some older kids "burn rubber."

Once parked, we exited her car and stood, looking at the water. Two egrets paused like flowers on the muddy edge of Goodwives River. At the very spot where it emptied into Gorham's Pond. Their black legs and beaks contrasted against their snowy white bodies. Fuzzy-topped cattails and blue-green rushes surrounded the birds, giving cover for their young.

As we merged with other teens at the foot of the hill, we craned our necks to view the upper classmates gun their engines and pop their clutches, peeling rubber as they twisted and spiraled up Long Neck Point Road, one by one. Seeing who could lay the longest black strip along the road. We stood riveted, staring at each racing car. The smell of salt air from the Sound, the acrid odor of engine oil, and the burning of rubber permeated the air. I recognized Don in his own souped-up car, a gold Studebaker, staring at the screeching cars. We heard squealing of tires and saw smoke shooting from under back fenders. Wheels slid across the tarmac. Gravel and dirt spewed in their wakes. We cheered the boys as they revved the engines and floored their accelerators.

After the finish of the noisy and exciting challenge, Elsa and I departed the crowd of kids. When her Mom's vehicle heaved its way up the slanting road, we marveled at the length of the dark marks on the pavement, the presence of burned rubber. At no time did we think of the lost tread and the consequent loss of money.

At the end of the road, gates stopped us from entering the Convent of the Sacred Heart, a private school for girls. Both Kathleen Kennedy, President-elect Kennedy's sister, and Charlotte Ford as well as her mother, Anne Ford from the Ford Motor Company family, attended the school. I mentioned that Anson Phelps Stokes built the three-story brick mansion in the early 1900s. Because he was a possible distant relative, I had learned about his mining, railroad, and banking interests, and that he allowed Andrew Carnegie to live there before an order of the Catholic Church bought the property.

When we returned to Rings End Road, we crossed its stone bridge, the three arches curving over Goodwives River. The nearby houses were some of the earliest dwellings in Darien. An area originally called Clock's Landing and then Gorham's Landing, with its grain mill and wharf trading center. In the early 1700s, merchant boats tied to the numerous rings on the quay, possibly revealing how Rings End Road obtained its name.

We spotted a trio of airborne ducks threading through the trees, flapping their wings and quacking as they flew. Gorham's pond, a home for recreational skaters in the winter, was a hotspot for numerous waterfowl in the summer.

# PORT CHESTER

The town of Port Chester was the place to party since New York State's drinking age was eighteen and Connecticut's was twenty-one. We could arrive at one of the many bars in half an hour, driving sixteen miles west from Darien on the Boston Post Road.

Roy picked me up the following Friday. A necker's knob embellished his steering wheel, a rotating round object attached to his driving wheel. It allowed him to place his right arm around my shoulders and still adequately maneuver his vehicle. On the bench seat of his Ford, he drew me closer as we drove through Stamford and Greenwich.

When he saw a car with only one headlight, he yelled, "Padiddle." He pulled his car to the side of the road, a smile on his face. I tilted my head back, closed my eyes, and gently parted my lips. Whoever shouted the word, "Padiddle" first got to kiss the person of the opposite sex. What a way to begin our date to Port Chester.

Although I didn't drink, I'd be ready to dance as soon as we hit one of the bars. When we entered a dark establishment along its main road, Roy walked to the counter, past fast-moving dancers, and ordered a beer and a coke. There was no room to sit, so we stood with our backs to the wall and watched the dancers. "Shake,

Rattle and Roll" blasted from the jukebox. The place was jumping. Swinging, twirling, twisting. Skirts flying, jackets waving, brows dripping. We placed our empty bottles in the bin and joined the mob on the floor. When a song by Elvis, "Falling in Love," came on, Roy took me in his arms. I glided inward, leaning my head on his chest.

All of a sudden, we heard raucous shouts, screaming swear words. As I turned toward the sounds, a green bottle flashed through the air, a beer bottle broken in half with blood falling from its sharp edges. Dancers scrambled to the side as two boys punched, fists striking faces and bodies. They rolled on the floor as lights flickered on and off. The music persisted.

"Let's get out of here!"

Roy grabbed my hand and hauled me out into the parking lot. We had just climbed into his car when we heard sirens and saw lights flashing, zooming toward us. Roy drove to the Post Road and rushed toward Darien. I twisted in my seat and looked out the back window. Three police cars poured into the parking area, their lights blazing. Patrons, hurrying from the bar, fled to their cars. Although the evening started out fine, almost perfect, it turned out to be terrifying. My first and only time at a bar in Port Chester.

# ZIEGLER ESTATE

I climbed into the backseat of the twins' blue Volkswagen, carrying my purse and scarf. As it was an exceptionally warm spring day when Sue and Nancy reached my house, their convertible top was down. I tied the silk scarf around my head and we maneuvered up Woodland to Nearwater and the Post Road. We followed Rings End Road to Pear Tree Point Beach, the place where Sue had been instructed to park. From there we boarded a school bus, skimming beneath tree limbs, their leaves vibrating as we were transported to the Ziegler Estate, our destination. Through granite pillars, past the stone gatehouse with its slate-shingled roof we entered Great Island. The main house, a stone structure studded with chimneys, stood a distance from the barn and stables.

"How'd they make their money?" I asked.

"Mom told me it was from baking powder. Weird, huh?" Sue said.

"And what about Steinkraus?" I asked. "He's that famous equestrian. You know, he's dating Helen Ziegler."

"No. I didn't know that. Are they getting married?"

"The rumor is next year but I'm not sure," I replied.

We chatted most of the way as the bus carried us to the carriage house. Droves of people from all over Fairfield and Westchester counties arrived for the annual secondhand event, put on by the Darien Auxiliary, specifically for the Children's Services of Connecticut. We called it the Children's Aid Sale.

The three of us walked across the cobblestone courtyard, through the arched entrance, and into the twenty-stall, granite stable and carriage house. I noticed the ceiling duplicated the herringbone tiles by Guastavino in the whispering gallery at Grand Central Terminal. What a place. And this was only for the horses.

Nancy spotted Gaysie and Janet with their mothers, checking out clothes nearest the barn's entrance. Each box stall was filled with used items to sell. Women's fashions crowded together with labels carrying such notable names as Dior, Chanel, and Cardin. Ballgowns and prom dresses from Bergdorf Goodman and Saks Fifth Avenue. Two stalls displayed men's clothes. Sweaters, suits, jackets, and tuxedos originally from the finest east coast stores. In the other stalls were hats and scarves, shoes, furs, jewelry, antiques, toys, books, and sports equipment. Even appliances. At the wide space at the far end of the barn stood rows of furniture and several oriental rugs. Outside were baked goods, lemonade, coffee, and tea. Even babysitting was provided. This was by no means your typical secondhand affair.

Gaysie and Janet joined us as we stalked the women's clothing, each of us finding a few things to bring home. I also examined the antiques and the twins checked the jewelry. I bought a blue blouse and a yellow hula hoop. Sue found a turquoise bracelet. Nancy picked out a cashmere Burberry scarf. We didn't buy much but we wanted to add to the event's fundraising benefit, supporting the children of Connecticut.

# SUGAR BOWL

The maple leaves had turned fiery, the sky a bright blue. Football season was in full swing. And the Darien team, the Blue Wave, was out in front. Winning every game so far for my senior year at high school.

"Give me a D," the head cheerleader, Hope, shouted to the teenage crowd stuffed into the Sugar Bowl, a breakfast and lunch business in downtown Darien. Wearing a white sweater and skirt, she stood on a chair and continued the cheer.

"D," we thundered back at her.

"Give me an A."

"A," we shouted. And so it continued until we had yelled all the letters of Darien. We had won another football game, expecting to be as good as Darien's undefeated teams of '56 and '57.

While we waited for the football boys to join our enthusiastic group, I sat on one of the red, vinyl-covered stools in front of the food counter. The Sugar Bowl always gave the Darien football team free sodas or floats with whipped cream if they won their game. Next to me sat Dawn, one of my ice skating buddies and a cheerleader. We talked about our numerous practices in her backyard, my learning the specific cheers; perfecting backbends, splits, cartwheels, and handstands.

Our conversation eventually turned to the Sock Hop, a dance in the high school gym the following Friday.

"Who was I going with? Would I wear plain socks or argyles?"

"Argyles, of course," I said. "And my green plaid skirt. It's pleated and has a large gold pin."

"I remember that," Dawn said. "I'll also wear argyles."

High schoolers continued to jam into the Sugar Bowl, jostling and pushing, clustering around the jukebox. Three songs for a quarter. Pushing buttons to make their selections. B2, D5, F3. They watched as a vinyl record was mechanically pulled from the stack and placed on a spinning turntable. "All I Have to Do is Dream" by the Everly Brothers. "At the Hop" by Danny and the Juniors. "Lucille" by Little Richard.

Jenny and Elsa joined us at the counter. They mentioned the time Doug Buchs's mother charged onto the field after a game and socked one of the opposing players. Some of us were in the stands and remembered the incident. Shocking to us all. Doug had told me the Harrison player was a dirty player and kept throwing mud into his brother's face. Into Butch's eyes.

"The player got kicked out of the game. But he returned in the second half. In a different jersey and number. Butch handled him anyway and Darien still won," Doug explained.

"That meant their coach instigated the switch of jerseys. The coach was in on it," I said.

"Yeah. You're right," he said. "When the game was over, Mom ran onto the field, right up to the Harrison player, and socked him squarely in the mouth. She only hit his face guard and probably hurt her hand. He still had on his helmet."

"I saw that. I couldn't believe it."

"The player was about to retaliate and punch my mother. Mr. Fraccola, a giant of a man, stood next to them. He's a local guy who weighed at least three hundred pounds. And was probably six foot five. He looked down at the Harrison player and said, 'Don't even consider it.'"

The drama ended and the opposing team's bus drove away, returning to its town in Westchester County, New York. Andre (Butch) Buchs was voted the first All State lineman from Darien.

# TOTS 'N' TEENS

"Jenny, Sue, Linda, and Mary Sue," I announced.

"No more. That's enough," Mom said. "Four girls plus you. That's plenty for a slumber party!"

"Okay. I'll call them and make it for eight o'clock. This Saturday, after dinner."

"Perfect. Remember you have to work that day."

As soon as Ginny left for college, I took her place on Saturdays running Tots 'n' Teens, a secondhand clothing store near the railroad underpass in downtown Darien. Mom recommended me for the job when none of the other volunteers wanted to work. I waited on customers, stocked shelves and racks, operated the cash register, dusted, and vacuumed. Whenever it was slow at the store, I perused the aisles, hoping to find something to buy. Invariably there was an article in my size and not too expensive. A dress or skirt or blouse. Exactly what I wanted to wear at school.

Mom, once again, was before her time. She was a supporter of Planned Parenthood, the beneficiary of Tots 'n' Teens. In 1960, Connecticut did not allow medical doctors to discuss any conception preventions with their patients, whether married or not. It was against the law. They could be fined or even jailed.

After the four girls arrived that evening, we assembled in the living room with sleeping bags, pillows, and overnight cases. Mom brought in a large bowl of popcorn and a six-pack of bottled Cokes along with a church key to help us pry off the lids. We sat in a circle on the carpet and threw bottle caps into Dad's wastebasket. I turned my transistor radio to Alan Freed's station. The New York channel hosted rock 'n' roll tunes, slow melodies, softly playing in the living room's background: "Sixteen Candles," "Save the Last Dance," "Can't Help Falling in Love."

"I worked at Tots 'n' Teens today. And I found a perfect dress. I'll wear it next week," I said as we listened to the music.

"What's it look like?"

"It's a navy blue madras," I answered. "By the way, have any of you heard of Planned Parenthood?" Puzzled looks and silence greeted my question. "Well, I found out that Planned Parenthood's the beneficiary of Tots 'n' Teens."

"No. Really? What's that?" Jenny asked, sitting on the carpet, leaning against the couch.

Since most of us were involved with Young Life, none of us was sexually active. That was one of Young Life's rules, to not have sex until you were married. However, we did hear about the "pill." It had just come on the market and everyone was talking about it. I told them as much as I knew about Planned Parenthood, about birth control and about doctors going to jail. My friends contemplated the significance of this startling new information, and after a long pause, I asked.

"Have any of you read *Peyton Place*?"

"Of course. Who hasn't?"

"Our parents think it's really about Darien. About wild alcohol and sex."

"If it's not about Darien, it could be," I said and then switched the subject, mentioning a classmate's recent accident.

"Jenny and I visited Tom in the hospital a few days ago. You knew he lost a toe, didn't you? While mowing between the library and the Red Cross buildings," I said. "There's quite a slope on the lawn and I guess he stepped into the blades."

"I went again with Elsa," Jenny said. "He certainly had a lot of visitors. It was like a party every time I went."

And so, the conversations changed and continued. We undressed and put on our pajamas, pink flowers or blue stripes, Mary Sue mentioned driving past Old McDonald's farm on the Post Road and going to the Norwalk Drive-In. *Where the Boys Are* with George Hamilton was playing at the outdoor theatre.

"What's it about?" I asked as I leaned against my dad's easy chair.

"Spring break on a beach in Florida," Mary Sue said. "I don't think my parents would allow me to go there when I'm in college."

We all agreed. No way would our parents allow us to drive to Florida without a chaperone. We were all pretty innocent.

"Did you see all those kids in Don's car?" I asked. "He told me he had four kids crammed inside his trunk."

"Didn't you have two in your trunk?" Jenny said. "I was in the front seat. Don't remember who was in the trunk."

"Who knows? Anything not to pay. I remember attaching the speaker to my window and praying I wouldn't forget it and drive away. Boy, would I be in trouble."

Just then, "Kansas City" came on the radio. I turned up the volume. We all stood and began to dance, swaying and twirling, singing and laughing. Jenny grabbed me and spun me under her arm, curling me and swinging me back to her. Being the tallest of our group, she decided to be the boy. I was her partner. When the song ended, we resumed our talks on the carpet and then took turns in the tiny bathroom under the staircase, brushing our teeth and washing our faces. When we returned to the living room, we reclaimed our seats, leaning on chairs, plunking down on the carpet.

"Speaking about getting into trouble, did any of you see the new floodlight on our garage?" I asked.

"What's that about?"

"If I stayed in a car too long, you know at the end of a date, my dad would flash the floodlight," I said. "In a second the front seat of my date's car became saturated in bright light. If I didn't get the hint, he'd flick the light on and off until I left the car."

"That's a riot," Linda said laughing.

We continued with our stories, mostly about boys. The traumas of dating and breaking up. Sometimes about other girls. Or about exams, or college, or sports. Our noise must have been too much.

"Okay, girls," my father called to us while standing in his striped pajamas on the upstairs landing. "Time for bed."

We crept into our sleeping bags, whispering to each other as we continued to talk. I reached over and turned off the lamp on the nearby side table. A gentle light glowed from the bathroom. Soft pillows cushioned our heads. Before long, all was quiet.

# JIM CROW LAWS

Tired from practicing softball, I left the field behind the high school and trudged to the school's parking lot. A fellow classmate, Kenny Smith, leaned against the hood of his car; his feet crossed out in front. He had on track shorts and a sleeveless racing shirt.

"What're you doin'?" I asked.

"Waiting for Scipio."

"Why?"

"I want to congratulate him."

"Why?"

"He's just been elected captain of the track team."

"Wow! Good for him!" Scipio was the only colored student in my class. To be chosen as captain of any team in an almost all-white school was quite an achievement.

"By the way, why's he in Darien? He and his sister are the only coloreds in our school."

Real estate agents knew how prejudiced Darien residents were. It was considered a "restricted" town. No coloreds and no Jews. That was the unwritten rule. Agents made exceptions for domestic help. And they discouraged people of Jewish heritage. "*Try Westport. They're more receptive.*" Even banks were involved. It was called "red-lining," a system used by loan officers to decide who should, or who should not, receive a home loan.

"His parents work for the Eng family. They have for years. You didn't know about the accident?

"No. What accident?"

"They're originally from South Carolina. They lived in a small cabin with no running water and no electricity. Before school Scip had to chop wood for the stove. After he brought logs into the kitchen, his younger sister, Essie, picked up the ax. She was only six."

"Oh, no! She didn't slice off a finger, did she?"

"No, but when she chopped on a log, a splinter broke off and jabbed her in the eye. It was actually sticking straight out."

"What happened?"

"Their parents raced to the local hospital but they wouldn't admit Essie because she was colored," Kenny said. "You know the South. It's filled with bigotry. Somehow, the parents notified the Eng family and they told them to come to Darien. They'd get her medical help. Scip's been here since the second grade."

"How's her eye?"

"She lost that eye, but kept the other. Scip told me an infection sometimes spreads from one eye to the other. She could have become blind. She was lucky."

"Hey, Scip," Kenny called as he saw him walking toward us.

"Hi, Scipio," I said.

"Congratulations!" Kenny said. "You'll be a great leader."

"Thanks, Kenny. I was really pleased with the vote."

"Are you caddying tomorrow?" Kenny asked.

"I caddy every chance I can. I need money for college."

"Did you get into UConn?" Kenny asked.

"Yeah. I can't wait."

"I was accepted, too," I said. "And into Syracuse. But my first choice is Pine Manor. I haven't heard back." I realized I sounded like I was bragging and asked another question.

"Where do you caddy?"

"Darien Country Club."

"We're members but we don't golf. Just tennis and swimming," I said. "Is there anyone special you caddy for? Like a movie star?"

"Most of the men are pretty serious, but one guy's great."

"Who's that?"

"Mr. Garrison. He's a division president with IBM. He laughs and jokes all the time. Really makes me feel good. He even asked me to apply to IBM after I graduate college."

"How super is that!" I said as I looked at my watch. "I have to go. See you guys tomorrow."

I turned and walked to my car. As I maneuvered my Chevy out of the parking lot, I saw the two boys still standing together. I rolled down my window and waved goodbye. I wondered; *Would he actually be hired by IBM?*

After dinner that night while lingering at the dining room table, I told my parents about Scipio Tucker and his little sister, Essie.

"She couldn't get into the hospital because of Jim Crow laws," Mom explained.

"If it's 'separate but equal,' they could have taken her to a hospital for colored people," I said.

"That's the law, Jim Crow laws, that is," Mom said. "But public facilities are often inferior, or not at all, for Negroes. There probably wasn't even a hospital nearby for the little girl."

Mom grew up in Bronxville, New York, but spent summers in Virginia. She also attended a boarding school in Charleston, South Carolina. She was very aware of the regulations created by Jim Crow laws. It surprised me that she didn't seem to be opposed to them. Maybe it was because she was a proud descendant of Robert E. Lee, Commander of the Confederate States Army. Mom had told us numerous stories about Lee — that he had graduated second in his class from West Point; that his first loyalty was to Virginia, not the United States; and that his horse, Traveller, was a gray saddlebred with a black mane and tail. Lee wrote the horse's name with two "Ls," the British way of spelling. Mom included "Lee" in my sister's name: Virginia Lee Phelps.

Neither of my parents nor any of our neighbors, it seemed, wanted people of color or of different religions living nearby. My parents had moved from Bronxville, another restricted town, where they preferred people with similar religions and races living near them.

Just a few hours earlier, Kenny and I had talked about the bias in the South. But we didn't have to drive ten hours south to find racial bigotry; it was thriving right in Darien. Not the kind of overt prejudice with people flying Confederate flags or hurling ethnic slurs, but with subtle approaches: realtors not allowing colored people to buy or rent in Darien, business owners not hiring colored staff, and school districts not employing colored teachers. *Someday*, I thought, *all this will change. Darien will be welcoming and progressive. It'll just take time.*

# MILLIE'S SECRET

Millie was a younger schoolmate who had moved away and had now returned to visit me. She parked in the turnaround of our driveway and carried her bulging suitcase into the house. Pretty and brown-haired, her full name was Mildred but no one called her that. She was staying for just one night and she came prepared. She had three changes of clothes, two books, make-up, toiletries, and pajamas. We had decided to see an early evening movie at the Darien Playhouse: *West Side Story* with Natalie Wood.

After Millie and I spent the obligatory fifteen minutes with my parents, she joined me in Mom's car. We drove out our driveway into town and parked on the Post Road, an extended distance from the theater. I knew boys would be driving by. Honking their horns and waving to us. It was Friday night. Time for cruising.

At the movie theater we bought popcorn and sodas and sat in the main area of the theater, middle seats, middle section. A balcony protruded behind and above us; that's where the "necking" kids sat. Soon the house lights lowered and two cartoons began. Then a newsreel started, depicting the latest political issues and society fashions.

Surrounded by crisp air-conditioning, we watched the West Side movie, New York gangs dancing on the big screen. With the beat of the music, we bounced in our seats and nodded our heads. When songs streamed from several speakers, we sang softly, turning to face each other.

"Hush!" Someone yelled behind us.

Giggling like typical teenagers, we quieted our words and leaned back in the leather seats. Our snacks disappeared while we watched the promising romance between the "Jet" boy and the "Shark" girl.

Feeling disenchanted with the outcome of the warring gangs, Millie and I left the theatre and strolled outside, alongside Grieb's Pharmacy and looked in their window. Elsa waved to us and peeked out the door.

"What'd you see?"

"*West Side Story*. Wish you didn't have to work."

"I couldn't get out of it."

"We'll catch you next time."

On the sidewalk we heard birds squawking, bickering with each other on a warm August evening. When we ambled along in dresses, underlined with netted crinolines, I was sure a few guys, passing in their cars, would stop to chat. And they did.

"Hey, Bobbi. Hey, Millie. Want to go for a ride?"

"Thanks but we have my car. How about meeting at the Tastee-Freez? That's where we're going."

Mom had loaned me her '57 Bel Air convertible. Turquoise with white-wall tires and tail fins, its gear shift alongside the steering wheel. After Millie climbed into the passenger seat, we put down the top, each of us releasing a latch above the front windshield. We were going to arrive in style.

The "Freez" was packed. Cars of all colors crowded around the building. Friends lingered near their highly polished vehicles. Sun sliced through trees, flashing off hood ornaments and chrome accessories. I parked in the lot and the two of us walked to the take-out window. We ordered hamburgers with lettuce and tomatoes and a side of French fries. *No onions, please.* A chocolate milkshake, topped with whipped cream, completed the meal. Our schoolmates converged around outside tables, calling to us.

Millie tended to be shy. This was a new experience for her. Once we had our meals in hand, we joined a group and listened to the latest gossip. After a few minutes of telling stories, one of the boys turned up the speaker in his convertible and loud music blasted around the Tastee-Freez. "Sherry" by Frankie Valli saturated the air. Sitting at one of the tables, we nodded our heads and tapped our feet to the beat of the music. My steady beau asked me to dance and I immediately jumped up. Millie's boyfriend, Jerry, hadn't arrived and she stayed on the two-person bench.

Then another song came on and then another. Swirls of skirts, swishing with the melody, dresses with wide cinch belts. Stockings with black leather flats. Our colorful scarves, trailing from around our necks, waved with the music. We danced "The Lindy," and swooped under our partner's arm, turning to swing back in front. A few others attempted "The Twist," a dance that had just been introduced on television's *American Bandstand*. They stood in one place, twisting their hips, knees and feet; bending forward and backward while twisting their bodies. Jerry finally showed up and instantly came to our table. It wasn't long before he and Millie began to dance. Slow and sweet to the sounds of "Teen Angel."

After an hour or so, we collected our purses and left for home. From my convertible we waved to the crowd. I turned right and drove to Nearwater Lane, past Hindley Elementary, and on to Woodland Drive. Once I parked in our garage, the two of us stumbled up the porch stairs, laughing as we entered the kitchen.

Mom greeted us with a wide smile and asked about the evening. We told her details of the movie and about dancing at the Freez. It was all we could do to keep from hyperventilating as we exploded with stories and funny descriptions. Exhilarated beyond belief.

"Don't stay up too late. We'll have breakfast at nine," Mom said.

After getting undressed to put on PJ's, we brushed our teeth and returned to my bedroom. In twin beds we lay facing each other, the nightstand between us. We didn't want to read. We wanted to talk.

"So, what's with you and Jerry?" I asked.

"We want to get married."

"What? What about college?"

"Oh, our parents won't let us get married. They say we're too young."

"Well, you are. Why don't you wait 'til after college?"

A few seconds passed and she lowered her head onto her pillow. Turning to face me, her face flushed scarlet.

"I have a secret. Promise you won't tell."

"Okay. I promise. What's so secret," I said as I leaned toward her.

Millie paused. She bit her bottom lip and didn't say a word. Raising onto her elbows and catching her breath, she finally spoke. It was only a whisper, but I heard the words.

"I had an abortion."

What? I couldn't believe it. I knew of no one who was even pregnant, let alone anyone who had had an abortion. This revelation came out of nowhere. I was completely caught off guard.

"My gosh! What happened?" I blurted out.

"You're the only one who knows besides Jerry and our parents. We wanted to get married but they refused to let us. They said it would ruin our lives. That's why we moved away."

"Where did you get an abortion? I thought it was illegal."

"It is. They found some place in Stamford, by the railroad tracks. My parents took me to a tenement building. Dad waited outside in the car but Mom came in," she said and paused again.

"I had to take off my panties and lie on a towel on top of a kitchen table. A colored woman stood by me and had me bend my knees. So tight, my heels touched my fanny. Then she placed a sheet over me. I heard a kettle boiling."

"Oh, Millie. You must have been so scared!"

"I was," she said as she caught her breath. "I raised my head and watched a man take a wire coat hanger and bend it. I lowered my head back to the table. I didn't want to watch. He pushed my knees outward and the woman firmly held them there," she said and hesitated.

"Then he shoved that thing into me." Her voice was so low I could hardly hear her.

"Mom started crying and grabbed my hand. "When he twisted the hanger, the pain was horrible. I couldn't stop screaming but that's all. I must have blacked out."

"I'm so sorry, Millie," I whispered as tears formed in my eyes. "Are you okay now?"

"I am, but just barely. I have awful cramps with lots of blood. My parents don't talk about it. In their mind, it's over. Jerry and I still love each other. But it's not the same."

Millie cried some more, tears dripping in a steady stream, spilling onto her sheet. She curled into a ball and moaned into her pillow, stifling her sobs. I heard her cry under her blankets. I could almost feel the sadness pulsating inside her. Millie's head and shoulders re-emerged and I reached over and gently squeezed her hand.

"Don't worry, Millie. Someday something special will happen. It might not be with Jerry, but you're pretty. You'll find someone else to love."

"Thanks, Bobbi. You're a good friend."

# COMMUTING

"May I sit here?" he asked.

Sitting next to the window on the New York/New Haven train, I turned and noticed there was no one else in the nonsmoking car. I had arrived early to catch up on some writing for a senior class. It was Friday and Darien had a teacher's conference. We had no school and I had been in the city to do some shopping. Dad would soon be on the same train, in one of the front smoking cars, playing bridge with his longtime cronies. I wore my best outfit, a Lanz two-piece suit with leather gloves.

"Of course," I said. I wasn't saving the seat and I didn't want to be rude to this gray-haired man.

*Why did he want to sit with me?* I thought. He could pick a seat from anywhere on the whole train. *Why me?* Then I realized it was April First, April Fool's Day. Dad was such a prankster, I wondered if he had set me up with one of his buddies. Well, I wasn't going to fall for it.

He placed his felt hat in the overhead rack, removed a newspaper from the crook of his arm, and squeezed himself in the train seat. He began to read and I continued my writing.

In another half hour, Connecticut commuters filled the car and I heard a conductor's whistle, signaling for the train to leave Grand Central Station. The train groaned and lurched as it pulled away and rattled forward on the city rails, crowded with men in dark suits, carrying evening newspapers.

Once the conductor collected our tickets, the heavy-set man leaned over me and pulled down the window shade. I continued writing a story that was sure to be published and ignored him. Then he reached over me again and raised the shade. His bulging belly slapped across my lined notepad, his breath reeking of liquor.

Our train left the dark terminal tunnel and bright sunlight slid into the passenger car as we passed several brick tenement buildings. In another few minutes, he again stretched over me, pulling down the window shade. As he drew back, he twisted his face to look at me and smiled. His bulbous nose was red and splotchy. I practically gagged. This was too much!

"Would you like to meet my father?" I said as I slammed papers back into my notebook.

"Yes, I would."

"Follow me. He's in one of the smoking cars."

He stood up and let me pass in front of him. The rough rocking and noisy clacking of the train continued. I opened the car door, walked gingerly through the dark passageway connecting the two passenger cars, and pushed open the door to the bar car. Passing the bartender and the stocked liquor counter on the left, I opened the next door and again crossed the loud coupling as it whined and grumbled, twisting and thumping. I pushed open the succeeding door and entered a smoking car.

Looking from side to side, I searched for my father. He always played bridge on his way home and always sat in one of the corner seats that were configured so four people could play cards. He was not there. The stocky man was still behind me, puffing as we walked. Going through the third coupling, I entered the last passenger car.

*Where was my father?* All I could see were newspapers held in front of faces. I started to panic. Sweat dripped down my back, soaking the slip under my suit. As I came to the last row of seats right before the engine, I saw my father calmly playing bridge. I rushed toward him, tears streaming down my cheeks. My father saw the terror in my face and stood to embrace me.

"I didn't hurt her!" the older man yelled behind me. Dad hustled me to his seat and grabbed the man by his lapels.

"What'd you do?" Dad shouted.

"Nothing," the man whined.

One of the bridge players, a lawyer, quickly rose and stood between the man and Dad. He pushed my father backward.

"Sit down, Jim," he commanded. He seized the portly man, turned him around, and shoved him away. The man waddled back toward his seat and vanished into the depths of the train. The bridge players stared at me.

"What happened?" my father asked.

"It's April First. I thought it was one of your jokes, Dad."

"What? I would never do anything like that."

"I know. But in the beginning, I thought it was a joke."

I explained in detail how the man had fallen across me several times, and none of the passengers had come to my rescue.

"Where are your papers and book?" Dad asked.

"Back at my seat along with a shopping bag."

"I'll get them, damn it."

"Now, Jim," said the lawyer. "No rough stuff. He could sue you if he got hurt."

"I'll be okay," he said as he turned and bolted toward the following passenger cars. When Dad came to the nonsmoking car, he saw the man sleeping, probably passed out. His fat belly protruded over his legs. Dad reached over the man's body and retrieved my book, bag, and papers. After he stood, he looked at the nearby men reading their newspapers.

"I can't believe it!" he shouted. "Not one of you tried to help my daughter. She was attacked by this jerk. Not one of you!"

The men lowered their papers and stared at my father. When he finished his angry tirade, they raised their hands and hid behind their newspapers, snapping the pages with urgency. *What was his problem?* They wondered. Dad was furious.

By the time he returned to me and his bridge-playing friends, I received the brunt of his anger. Since I had not been hurt, he became upset by the scene I had caused. That I had embarrassed him. I sat with my head bowed and listened to his lecture. He finally calmed down and the bridge game continued. It was important for his daughters to be accepted by the rules of society. Never were we to create a negative situation. I knew that and learned April First was not always a "Fool's Day."

# SENIOR PRANKS

On Fridays, we exploded from school as if we had been propelled from a cannon, racing to our cars, hugging books to our chests. After spring break and before final exams, the weekend was ours. Time for flashy antics, for tasteless clowning, for tricking our schoolmates.

One of the more popular pranks high school guys accomplished was to pee off a Merritt Parkway Bridge. The designated boy had to have a strong flow, one that could fly up and over the concrete railing, and fall to the highway below, hopefully hitting a passing vehicle.

"Okay. Ready? Go!"

The boy had to be prepared. His aim had to be straight. If it weren't, many a teen standing "watch," was accidentally hit by a stray stream of urine. Lots of laughter, lots of excitement. Except for anyone passing underneath the bridge. Especially driving in an open convertible.

A few years earlier, a group of senior boys staged a panty raid at the water-edged convent at the end of Long Neck Point Road. They came by boats and pulled a downed tree to the privacy gate, keeping police from entering the school grounds. While cavorting with the dorm girls, the boys gathered several panties. Alarms were set off. Sirens bounced off interior walls. Girls ran back to their rooms. The boys sprinted to their boats and raced into the Sound. The raid was famous; the police were embarrassed. And no boaters were caught.

─────────

In my sister's 1959 class, there was a renowned gathering at Weed Beach. It happened a few weeks before graduating. It was supposed to be an early morning breakfast party, hosted by a group of senior girls. A band of boys, classmates of the girls, crashed the party, bringing with them a radio and cartons and cartons of beer. After much drinking and dancing in the sand, everyone left for school.

As soon as they arrived, the teachers began to suspect something. One boy crawled along the hallway, muttering as he attempted to reach his homeroom class. Another fell off his chair and lay on the floor, moaning and holding his head. And still another boy raced to the men's room, clasping his hand across his mouth, vomiting as he ran.

Principal Atkinson called the obvious drunks to his office and asked who else was at the beach party. About thirty boys were named. When they were each summoned to his office, he asked one question.

"Have you been drinking?"

Fifteen boys answered, "Yes." Fifteen boys were expelled. The *Darien Review* picked up the story as did the *New York Times* and the *New York Herald Tribune*.

Parents were furious. *If their sons didn't graduate, could they still attend college?* Owing to extreme pressure from the teens' parents, Superintendent Chubbuck gave the boys a reprieve. They would be expelled for two weeks in spite of breaking school rules and Connecticut State laws. And yes, they would be allowed to graduate with their class.

Half a dozen boys waited out their time at another maverick's house. They met each school day, playing poker, eating potato chips, drinking sodas, and reminiscing about their actions. Supposedly they were learning math, figuring out the odds on the numbered cards. And just maybe, they thought about the consequences and possible repercussions of their morning of drinking at Weed Beach that fateful day.

―――――――

My own class accordingly honored the senior tradition and accomplished a prank of its own. Five boys gathered after the prom and piled into Gene's convertible, a 1950 chartreuse Ford. He was my snowball-fighting neighbor from Beach Drive. It was way past midnight, about two in the morning, yet they still wore their prom jackets and slacks. They had planned to cut down a tree the junior class had planted. The previous year, the seniors had chopped our class tree and tossed it on top of the high school.

As the boys drove around the parking lot, they noticed the appointed tree, about eight feet tall, with a plaque commemorating the donation. Alan, sitting in the shotgun seat, jumped out and used a handsaw to cut the tree in half. Noticing another car at the school, he quickly threw the top portion into the nearby woods and raced back to Gene's convertible, flying over the door, landing in the passenger seat. Gene's car, its florescent green paint shining in the parking lot, was easily identified. The following Monday, the assistant principal and later the guidance counselor grilled the boys. They were afraid of being expelled and not graduating. They stayed true to their word. They never confessed.

# DEBUTANTE PARTIES

After the senior prom and high school graduation with its *Pomp and Circumstance*, the debutante season began. In Darien, that was when we had the most teen parties, the most fun gatherings, and the time I most wanted to be a debutante. Instead, I participated at the deb parties as a guest, without any expenses for my parents. But it was not the same. I couldn't wear a white dress and have my father escort me at the cotillion. I couldn't call myself a "debutante." Still immature at eighteen, I equated wealth and its trappings with appreciation and acceptance.

All summer the parents of the Darien debutantes gave parties at their homes, their clubs, their private beaches. I lay on the sand at Weed Beach, tanning one side and flipping over to tan the other. Bronzing my body to be desirable to the boys at the many festivities. A row of girls, also getting ready for the numerous parties, joined me in the ritual, lying side by side on colorful towels. Some added peroxide to their hair, intensifying their newly-bleached streaks of bright yellow against their naturally dark hair. It was all we could do to keep from laughing at our attempts to be attractive, to be popular.

Lester Lanin, famous for long, smoothly arranged medleys, played at several of the debutante parties. In Westchester and Fairfield counties, and even on Long Island. Throughout the evening he'd toss red baseball caps with his name embossed across the brim. It was a token everyone wanted. During one of the deb parties in Greenwich, Sue reached out and grabbed a cap before her twin sister could even think about it. A special souvenir for her fun-filled evening.

Parents of my friends hosted a Hawaiian Dinner Dance at the Tokeneke Club that late August. It was the largest of the celebrations. Seven debutantes, numerous escorts, and masses of guests filled the club's event room, located on a sandy beach with waves lapping at its shore. Perfect for a luau party. Bright lights wrapped around poles, draped from the tops of walls, and covered the palm-decorated bar. Boys wearing flower-printed shirts leaned on the bar, surveying the seven debs who had decorated themselves in thick white leis. As I entered, Jenny placed a colorful lei around my neck. Her brother stood nearby and asked me to dance. Susie, Marilyn, and Mary were already on the dance floor with their escorts. A live band, rock 'n' roll music at its finest, played from a corner of the room. There on the teak floor twirled a guy in an unusual Hawaiian outfit: half coconuts for a bra and a skirt made of grass strands, dancing with anyone who would welcome him in his strange get-up.

Alcohol flowed. Layers of leis were added to the participants: around ankles, wrists, necks. Barefoot dancing, gaiety, and laughter. Tipsy teens and a few parents waded into the waters, holding their glasses high, howling at the fun they were having. At the best party of the season.

As the summer waned, the debutantes and their families gathered for the autumn cotillion. The event marked the official joining of a young lady to society.

Steeped in tradition and rituals, the celebration was also about fostering community activities and supporting charity. Darien's cotillion benefited the nearby hospitals in Stamford and Norwalk.

In early September parents, escorts, and debutantes gathered at the Wee Burn Country Club. When the cotillion began, each debutante glided with her father toward the cotillion committee to be "presented to society." She curtsied and bowed, holding her father's hand. The dads wore formal ensembles: black tailcoats, white shirts, white waistcoats, and white bow ties with black trousers and freshly-polished, patent-leather shoes. White gloves completed their outfits. How handsome they looked, these debutante fathers.

The debutantes wore floor-length white gowns, tight around the waist, with layers of crinolines underneath. White kid gloves rose above their elbows and many added a string of pearls with matching earrings. Each young woman carried a bouquet of white flowers with green vines draping from the arrangement. After the end of the grand presentations, the debutantes began to dance. First with their fathers and then with their escorts. To the big band music played by the club's local group. Songs from Tommy Dorsey, Glenn Miller, Benny Goodman. This was an evening they all would remember, the time they were accepted into society.

# COLLEGE BOUND
Summer of 1961

# SAILING IN THE SOUND

Restlessness surged through me. *What should I do after college? Would the Peace Corps accept me? Should I work in New York City? Or maybe California?* Round and round my questions went, whirling in and out of my mind, crowding my brain. For today, my plans were to go sailing.

I had my brown hair tied back in a ponytail and wore a turquoise bikini. I was excited to be invited on this daylong cruise with my latest boyfriend. Bill and a half dozen of his classmates from Williams College had invited dates for a planned venture to a specific cove along New York's Long Island. We sailed in an impressive ship, complete with engine, dining, and living rooms. Five of the boys were knowledgeable sailors. Bill was not. We watched them as they rigged the ship, tied knots, and raised the mainsail, fastening the jib at the very front.

It was almost noon when the *Midnight Manor* sailed from the Noroton Yacht Club, past Pratt Island, and into Long Island Sound. Halyards clanked against masts as we made our way east, speeding through tunnels of sunlight and shadows. Chains and hinges snapped in our wake. Bells pealed as the two-masted sailboat tipped nearby buoys.

I leaned over the ship's railing and spotted the land of Long Island, looming on the far-off horizon. Bill stood beside me, his arm around my waist, pulling me closer. A few boats emerged and then vanished, rising and falling on distant swells. Gulls flew overhead, dipping and disappearing, reappearing with new finds of wriggling fish. The loud concussive pop of a sail, filling and snapping taut in the wind, burst through the air. We were sailing at a fast clip thoroughly enjoying the journey.

After an hour or so of sailing up the Connecticut coast and crossing the Sound, we glided into a cove and anchored. Time for swimming. Then lunch and beer. I noticed the blond hair on one of the girls, cascading over her shoulders, blowing in the breeze. How gorgeous she was. And how Bill kept staring at her. Jealousy surged through me. His friends were only a year or two older than I was, but in their minds, we were worlds apart. The girls attended Smith, Skidmore, and Mt. Holyoke. I had just graduated high school.

As the afternoon wore on, we began our journey back to Darien. Bill sat cross-legged in a circle on the deck, playing cards, ignoring me. I had had enough. I tiptoed behind him, holding a pitcher of ice-cold water. While he leaned forward to place a card, I poured the freezing water down the back of his shirt.

"Shit!" Bill yelled as he jumped from the teak floor and raced after me. After he caught me, he wrapped my squirming body in his arms and held me close to his chest. I laughed and folded my arms around him. Finally, I had his attention.

He undid my hands from around his neck, raising me high above his head, and tossed me over the boat's railing. My foot caught the horizontal rail and slammed my body into the side of the sailboat. My feet snapped over my head and I continued my graceless plunge into the rough waters. For a moment, the air was knocked out of me. Once I gained the surface, my head above the swells, I saw the blue sailboat passing me by.

"Grab the rope," Bill yelled.

I swam to the painter, trailing a hundred feet behind the sailboat, and held on. Or tried to. The rope whipped through my hands, burning my palms as it rushed onward. A large knot had been tied at the end and I clasped it, hanging on with all my strength, waves splashing against my face, forcing seawater into my eyes and mouth. Bill and his friends hauled me toward the boat as it continued to surge through the Sound, dragging me rapidly behind the boat. By the time I reached the stern of the boat, the top of my bathing suit was around my neck and the bottoms were at my knees.

"Don't pull yet," I yelled from a small platform in the rear of the boat, still gagging from all the water I had swallowed. With as much dignity as possible, I repositioned my bathing suit. Once I said, "Okay. Pull," my eyes never left Bill as he and the others began to drag me upward.

My legs and arms ached. I was exhausted. Bill hauled me over the highest railing and I collapsed; my knees buckling, no longer strong enough to stand. My whole body felt numb. Hands, feet, chest. I couldn't feel a thing. He lifted me, binding me in his arms and pressing me to him, a cocoon around my shaking body. I started to cry. My emotions came over me like a pipe bursting. I couldn't stop crying.

"I'm so sorry. That was stupid of me. Really stupid," he whispered. The terror in my stomach subsided. I leaned my head against his chest and slowly calmed. He gripped the back of my neck and pulled my face closer, reeling me in for a soft, smooth kiss.

The others shuffled away, venturing back to sailing and card games. Bill and I moved to the railing, staring at the water as we continued our trip back to Darien, the sun dropping toward the horizon, just beginning to set. In the silence that followed, he blurted out that he wanted to see more of me. Wanted me to go with him to Manhattan next Saturday. Wanted me to visit him at Williams. My immature prank proved rewarding. Risky, true. But still rewarding.

# LEAVING DARIEN

Growing up in Darien meant I, unconsciously, felt entitled to certain jobs, to live a certain way, to date certain men. I was confident yet unaware of my privilege. To me, it was normal. I never knew anything different. Within a week of high school graduation, Pine Manor accepted me. I continued to date Bill on and off that year. Enjoying each other but not committing to a steady relationship.

In 1963, eleven Darien girls sailed on Cunard's Queen *Elizabeth 1* for a chaperoned European excursion. After a one-month tour through England and Europe's mainland, six of us continued our explorations for an additional two weeks. I hitchhiked to Copenhagen, the capital of Denmark, with a Princeton student I had met earlier on the Cunard ocean liner. That European voyage was the beginning of my taste for international travel.

I adored Darien; its history, the New England seasons, and my special friends. But it was time to move on. I no longer wanted to have my life planned for me. I wanted to discover unique cultures, to experience distinct adventures, and to explore new countries. My parents agreed with a California relocation and sadly sent me on my way, giving me the opportunity to develop my talents and to blossom.

# EPILOGUE

"Risky but rewarding" behavior was the essence of my life. My exuberant explorations started when I discovered our neighbor's pond in Darien. After my family moved from Leroy Avenue to Outlook Drive, my precarious conduct continued: running away, examining a winter pond, climbing to the peak of our house. To me, obstacles meant opportunities. A chance to learn, to challenge, to investigate.

After attending the executive course at Katharine Gibbs Secretarial School in Manhattan, I drove to San Francisco and became a legal secretary at Pillsbury, Madison & Sutro. After fourteen months, I decided I'd rather travel. I no longer wanted to be a secretary.

I applied to an international airline company. Only fifty percent of those admitted to the training program were chosen. I was accepted and for six years I took troops to Europe and the Orient, specifically to Vietnam. During the height of the war our plane was shot at, the runway was damaged by mortar fire, and we had to hide in bunkers until the shelling stopped. I wrote about this eye-opening time of my life in the book, *Behind the Smile during the Glamour Years of Aviation*.

Following my years as a flight attendant, I decided to roam the world by myself. In doing so, I became the only

American tourist in Cairo, accidentally arriving two days before Israel deployed crippling airstrikes against Egypt during the Six-Day War. I was locked up for five days in the Hilton Hotel and then transported to the coastal city of Alexandria where I and 566 men were rescued by the U.S. Sixth Fleet. I joined diplomats, businessmen, and media personnel crossing the Mediterranean to Greece.

When I later ventured for a second time around the world, I incurred frightening challenges while working in the Middle East. I wrote about my journey in *Black Empress, Rescuing a Puppy from Iran*, a tale of affection and intrigue.

Thanks to the encouraging attributes passed on by my mother, I challenged the norm and explored the world. My father guided and enlightened me. My sisters influenced and encouraged me. And through all my adventures, an angel protected me from my risky but rewarding behavior, beginning as a toddler when I first dipped my toes in Darien waters.

# POSTSCRIPT

The following notes are in the order they appeared in *Darien Waters*:

Census: In the 1940 census, fifty people of color were listed in Darien; all were hired help and their families. The town's population was less than 9,000. By 1960, the population was 18,000.

Sleep Tight: In Colonial times, most people had rope beds. The expression "sleep tight" came from the use of those beds. The tighter the ropes, the firmer the foundation, the easier it was to sleep.

Dungarees: A material from India, thus the name. The work pants eventually were named "blue jeans," and then just "jeans."

Horseshoe Crabs: Horseshoe crabs are not crabs at all. They are more associated with spiders than with crabs. They acquired their name from the shape of their helmet. It looks like a horseshoe. Today their blood, which is blue, is used to test vaccines for harmful bacteria. A half million crabs have their blood harvested once a year. Afterward, they are returned to the ocean where they can live up to twenty years.

Nancy Drew: The Nancy Drew Books depicted a teenage detective solving one mystery after the other. Its author,

Carolyn Keene, was a pseudonym for numerous male and female writers.

The Noroton Yacht Club: It was constructed entirely of wood in 1928. During Hurricane Sandy in 2012, extensive damage ensued. The members voted to replace it with a building that could withstand hurricanes and fires.

Cabbage Night: Cabbage Night came from the custom among young Scottish women of examining cabbages pulled from their neighbor's garden on the night before Halloween to see what their future husbands would look like. Once they performed this bit of witchcraft, the girls threw the cabbage against their neighbor's door and ran away, marking the beginnings of many pre-Halloween pranks. Nationally called "Mischief Night."

The Nickerson House: Henry Davis Weed built the house as his summer home. His main residence was in Savannah, Georgia. Mr. Nickerson, a Manhattan attorney, purchased the home from the Weed family in the late 1920s. He is the one who subdivided the home's original property (hence, Darien has Nickerson Lane, a road that wraps behind the house.)

Hasidic Jews: One of the best books on the subject is *Unorthodox* by Deborah Feldman, about a Jewish girl who gives insight into the rules of Hasidic Jews.

The Presbyterian Property: Lewis Clock, a farmer, made the land available for the development of the First Presbyterian Church in 1864. Benjamin Weed was the primary founder of the church. He lived on the Post Road next to Garden Gate where his good friend, Frederick Bruggerhof, resided. Carrie Bruggerhof Hodges lived on the corner of Noroton Avenue and the Post Road and later gave her house to the church. It was occupied by the associate minister, Laird Miller, and his wife. They allowed me to keep my horse in their barn behind the house.

Helen (Sis) Ziegler: Known as the "Grande Dame of Dressage," she grew up in both Manhattan and Great Island. In spite of her extreme wealth, she became active in Darien's Post 53 Ambulance service where she qualified as an EMT-1. In 1960 she married William (Bill) Steinkraus. He was from Westport, Connecticut, and graduated from Yale. At the 1968 Summer Olympics in Mexico, he won a gold medal in individual jumping with the horse, Snowbound. Great Island, the 63-acre Darien estate, originally went on the market for $175 million. It's currently listed at $120 million.

Scipio Tucker: In the face of widespread allegations of rampant racial prejudice in Darien, a group of athletes elected Scipio Tucker captain of their track team. After high school, Scip graduated from the University of Connecticut, majored in mathematics and statistics, and lettered in football and track. He spent a year in Vietnam as an officer and was awarded both a bronze star and a purple heart. After his tour of duty, he approached Mr. Garrison at IBM, and true to his word, Mr. Garrison opened doors for Scip to apply. Scipio worked thirty years at IBM, finishing as a Program Manager of Executive Resources in the Information Systems Department. His sister, Essie, returned to Darien after college and taught elementary classes in Darien until she married. Her children are all college graduates, one of whom has two PhDs and an MD as an orthopedic surgeon. They both thank the Darien school system for their education and for their families' scholastic successes.

<u>Prejudice in Darien</u>: The Ku Klux Klan preached a doctrine of Protestant control of America and suppression of Negroes, Jews, and Catholics. A Darien resident, Harry Lutterman, was Connecticut's Grand Dragon in 1925. *Gentleman's Agreement*, a novel by Laura Hobson, depicts a journalist who poses as a Jew to research anti-Semitism, an exposé on the unwritten covenant that prohibited real estate sales to Jews in Darien.

<u>Comstock Law</u>: Any type of birth control could see their users fined or sent to jail. There was equal punishment for anyone "aiding and abetting." Doctors or pharmacists could be punished for providing birth control devices or any information about birth control. Since 1844, the Comstock law applied to anyone in Connecticut that prevented conception.

<u>Griswold vs. Connecticut</u>: In 1961, just a year after the "Pill" hit the shelves, two birth control advocates spearheaded an act of civil disobedience in response to Connecticut's Comstock law. Estelle Griswold, the executive director of the Planned Parenthood League of Connecticut, and Dr. C. Lee Buxton, the chair of the Department of Obstetrics at Yale University's medical school, opened a birth control clinic — and were promptly arrested, prosecuted, and fined $100 apiece for defying state law. During the clinic's brief lifespan, from November 1 to 10, married couples received counseling, exams, and birth control prescriptions — all in violation of state law. Ms. Griswold immediately challenged the constitutionality of Connecticut's anti-contraception law but it was upheld in state courts. It found its way to the Supreme Court, which, in a 7 to 2 decision, ruled that married couples had a constitutional right to make

private decisions about contraception. The ruling was limited to married couples only.

<u>Darien Parties</u>: In 1964, seventeen-year-old Nancy Hitchings was killed while driving home from a party with her escort. The accident happened after a gala hosted by Darien parents who had served liquor to minors. They were subsequently sued. From that time on, liquor rules were strictly enforced. Liquor was allowed only to those twenty-one and over.

# THE AUTHOR

Bobbi Phelps grew up in Darien, Connecticut, and graduated from Darien High School in 1961. She received an Associate of Arts degree from Pine Manor College. Before graduating from the University of California at Berkeley with a Bachelor of Arts degree, she was employed as a legal secretary in San Francisco. In 1965 she became an international flight attendant.

Bobbi started the Angler's Calendar and Angler's Catalog Companies in 1975. In 1993 her calendar company won Exporter of the Year for the State of Idaho (small business category).

Bobbi was a twenty-year member of the Outdoor Writers Association of America, a nine-year Idaho board member for The Nature Conservancy, an Arnold Gingrich Writers recipient from Fly Fishers International, a five-star award winner from Literary Titans, and a first-place gold medalist from Feathered Quill Book Reviews.

When Bobbi retired and married Larry Chapman (Darien High School Class of 1959), she began to write books. They moved to Tennessee and the Authors Guild of Tennessee twice voted her president.

Her website is www.booksbybobbi.com.

Her email address is bobbiphelps1@gmail.com.

# ACKNOWLEDGMENTS

Besides the internet, one of the best places to find information about the history of Darien, is reading *The Story of Darien, Connecticut* by Kenneth M. Reiss. From the time of Native Americans to present-day locals, he filled in the gaps with abundant accounts, pictures, and documents.

Another wonderful source came from the Darien Library, specifically from Blanche Parker in the resource department. Whenever I had questions about a certain event, she emailed me article after article to verify and enrich the story. I can't thank her enough!

I am forever grateful to my writing and reading friends who edited *Darien Waters* from its earliest conception to its final form: Cheryl Adamkiewicz, Janet Fitzsimons, Susan Kite, Cheryl Peyton, and Susie Nims Scott. Lynn Toettcher pushed me to include sections I had planned to eliminate and to write a conclusion. My sister, Ginny Phelps Clemens, oversaw the family narratives and stayed by my side through every step of the writing process, using her skills as an author herself to tweak the passages to be their very best. All of them were invaluable to me with their corrections and suggestions. I am indebted and humbled by the role Kathy Economy and Tilmer Wright, Jr., undertook, nudging me to write a better book by sharpening the manuscript to its final state. And I am blessed to be married to Larry Chapman who surrounded me with encouragement as I tackled this challenging project.

The following Darien schoolmates assisted me with specific stories and with validating tales I had previously heard: Gay (Gaysie) Lloyd Franklin Best, Holly Blake, Jack (Pat) Cataldo, Gail Phelps Champlin, Mary Sue Young Christoffers, Dawn Whelan Cerbone, Gary Cosman, Sue Bellamore Damour, Mary Towne Doten, Janet Fitzsimons, Pete Friedman, Rob Johnston, Linda Stone Kemp, Alan Learch, Rosemary Hull Mace, Winnie Carlson Mead, Dottie Daddona Merrill, Don Millspaugh, John Monroe, Ken Rawn, Jan Strauss Raymond, Sandy Sarhatt-Pear, Mark Schoenwald, Susie Nims Scott, Sally Smith, Essie and Scipio Tucker, and Elsa Lane Williams.